GCSE Success

AQA

English
Language & Literature

Revision Guide

Complete
Revision & Practice

Ian Kirby
and
Paul Burns

Contents

Purpose, Audience, Form: PAF

➤ While you're reading a text, you should try to identify its purpose, audience and form.
➤ This will help you to understand how and why the author is writing in a certain way.

Purpose

➤ To understand a text, you need to know what it's doing.
➤ The three texts below are written to inform, persuade and instruct.
➤ Other purposes include argue, advise, describe, explain and review.
➤ You should revise the specific features of writing styles. (A good way to do this is by practising your writing using different styles. See pages 26–33.)

1

DAILY NEWS

World · Business · Finance · Lifestyle · Travel · Sport · Weather

Issue: 240104   THE BEST SELLING NATIONAL NEWSPAPER   Est - 1965

First Edition   Monday 5th June

Arson at Hospital

Fire workers, yesterday, fought to control a blaze at St Martin's Hospital in Westbury. Police are treating the fire as arson.

2

Hi Mum!

Everything's going well at uni – but I've run out of money! I'm literally living on beans (no toast, it's got that bad). I'm really really sorry but could you just send me £20 to get me to the end of the week?

Cheers Mum, love you lots,

Rach x

3

Perfect Scones

250 g self-raising flour
50 g butter
1tsp baking powder
1 egg
100 ml milk

Cut the butter into small chunks and gently work it into the flour and baking powder until it feels like breadcrumbs.

Mix in the milk and whisked egg to create a dough, then roll out to a thickness of about 3 cm.

Formal ➤ behaving or writing in a serious or respectful manner.
Informal ➤ being more friendly or relaxed.

Audience

➤ It's important to think who a text is written for, as this will affect how it has been written.

➤ In the texts opposite, the first one is for anyone interested in the news (but aimed at adults). The second one is specifically to Rachel's mother. The last one is for people who like cooking and want to know how to make scones.

➤ The audience will affect whether something is **formal** or **informal**.

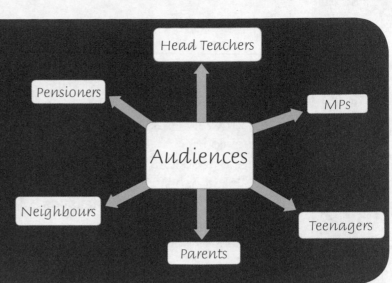

Period

➤ You should also think about when the text was written.

➤ One of the texts you will be given will be modern (written in the 20th or 21st century) like the ones opposite.

➤ The other text will be older, written in the 19th century.

➤ Older texts will often be more formal, contain longer sentences, and use more unusual and old-fashioned vocabulary.

Form

➤ You should also think about the form of writing that you've been given: what is it or where would it be found?

➤ The texts opposite are a newspaper article, an email and a recipe. Each will have been written differently because of what it is.

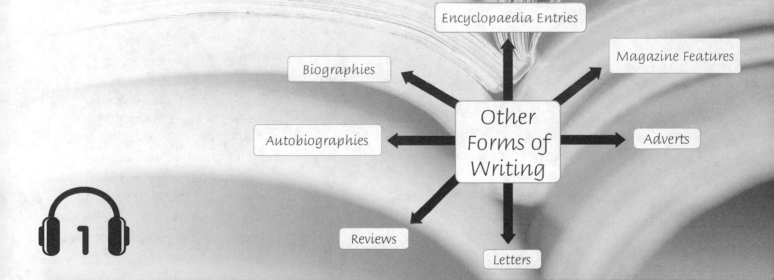

Get a magazine (and any junk mail you've been sent) and cut out different examples of texts. Stick them to a sheet of A3 and identify their purpose, form and audience. To develop your skills, underline parts of each text that have helped to reveal the PAF.

What does PAF stand for?

What different writing purposes are there?

What different audiences might you encounter?

What different forms might a text be written in?

Module 1   Purpose, Audience, Form and Period

Retrieving Facts

➤ Facts are things that can be proven by evidence.

➤ For example: "49 per cent of the people said they like peas." is a fact. However: "Peas taste horrible." is an opinion.

➤ It's a good idea to look for names or titles (these stand out because they use capital letters), or **statistics** (which stand out because they are numbers). These are all facts.

> The first question in this exam will be in the form of a list of statements. You will be asked to show, by ticking boxes, which of them are true according to the text.

Retrieving Opinions

➤ Opinions are things that people think or feel about something. They are personal rather than based on evidence.

➤ You can start by looking out for speech marks. These will show you when someone is giving their personal view (such as an interview in a newspaper).

➤ You should also look out for **adjectives** that offer a judgement, such as words like good, bad, tasty, horrible, etc.

Quoting

➤ Remember to keep your quotations brief and relevant.

➤ Selecting a few words is much better than copying out several lines.

Synthesis

➤ Synthesis means combining information from more than one source.

➤ In your second question, you will be asked to summarise differences and/or similarities between the two texts.

➤ The question will have a particular focus.

➤ You could be asked to compare the writers' opinions. Do not comment on them or say which you prefer.

➤ Remember only to write about the contents of the texts.

➤ Do not comment on the writers' style or techniques.

➤ Make sure you write about both texts equally.

Summarising

➤ Summarising is all about retrieving the main points in a text.

➤ You need to write these ideas in your own words to show you actually understand.

➤ The best way to find main points is to think what the whole text is about, then re-read the beginning of each paragraph. Often, a writer will use a topic sentence to introduce their main idea.

➤ You will need to use **connectives** to show sequence (e.g. firstly, then, finally), addition (e.g. also, furthermore) and possibly contrast if there are different views to summarise (e.g. however, in comparison).

Decide what the whole text is about.

Re-read the opening sentences of each paragraph.

Statistics ➤ information based on the collection of data.
Adjectives ➤ describing words.
Connectives ➤ words that help to join ideas in different ways.

Quickly make a list of similarities and differences and number these to give a logical order.

Underline any main points that you find.

Do the same for the second text.

Write out the main points in your own words, joining them with suitable connectives.

Find any news article and two highlighter pens. Choose one colour for facts and another for opinions, and highlight the article. To develop your skills, try this again with a different purpose article such as a review. (Do you find more or less opinion? Why might this be?)

What is a fact?
What is an opinion?
Where is the best place to find the main points of a text?
Why should you use your own words when summarising?

Features of Language
➤ Try to use technical terms for features of language, for example: verb (doing word), adverb (word that describes a verb), etc.
➤ Try to identify any specific techniques, for example: **rhetorical question, second person, repetition,** etc.
➤ Think about why the writer has used certain words or techniques.

Language and Purpose
➤ When analysing why the writer has included certain language, you need to consider the purpose of the text. For example:

You're going to love this little gadget – it will change your life!

Purpose		Language		Effect
Persuade	→	Repeated second person (you)	→	Grabs the reader's attention
Persuade	→	Emotive verb (love)	→	Suggests gadget is great
Persuade	→	Alliteration (l)	→	Makes key words stand out

➤ What you might write:

The writer makes repeated use of the second person as a persuasive technique. Repeating 'you're'/'your' catches the reader's attention, making them feel special and think the product could benefit them.

This is added to by the emotive verb 'love' which persuades the reader that the product is so amazing that they will make an emotional connection with it.

To highlight this, the writer also uses alliteration to persuade, 'love, little, life'. This makes key words stand out: emphasising the emotional connection, how compact it is, and implying a positive effect on the reader's lifestyle.

Sentence Structures for Effect
You should look out for ways in which punctuation can help achieve the writer's purpose. For example:
- short sentences to emphasise information
- lists to build up details
- exclamation marks to highlight a point
- colons to create a pause and emphasise a fact.

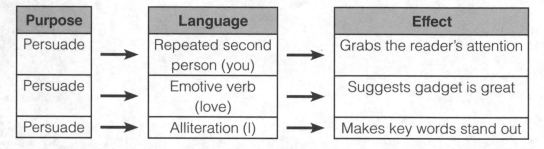

Text Structure

➤ Think about how information is structured to meet its purpose. Consider the start, middle, and end:

  ➤ How does the opening grab the reader and establish the purpose of the text?

  ➤ How does the ending bring the writing to a close and try to achieve some lasting effect on the reader?

  ➤ What features of structure are used to meet the purpose in the rest of the text? For example:

    ➤ Do topic sentences establish the main point of each paragraph?

    ➤ Are connectives used to show the reader the direction a text is taking?

    ➤ Does the message of the text develop or change?

    ➤ Does the type of writing change, for example by using more facts or greater description?

Rhetorical question ➤
a question that is used to make the reader think.
Second person ➤
writing or speaking to your audience directly, using 'you'.
Repetition ➤
using important words more than once to reinforce your meaning.

Make cue cards for different technical terms, such as adjective or second person. Write the term on the front and the definition on the back. Scatter them around the house (although this may annoy the other people you live with!) and, each time you see one, test yourself. To develop this skill, buy some different coloured sticky dots. Allocate a feature of language to a colour and stick them all over a magazine you're reading, each time thinking about the effect of the feature you've identified.

What is a verb, a noun, an adjective, and an adverb?

What features of sentence structure might you look for in a text?

What areas should you think about when exploring how a text is structured?

Reading the Question

➤ Read the question carefully so you know what you need to specifically compare.
➤ You will usually be given a theme, such as animals, the environment, etc.
➤ You will be given prompts reminding you to compare the writers' attitudes and the methods they use to convey those attitudes. You will also be reminded to use quotations from both texts.

What to Include

Come up with a similarity or difference about how the writers approach the theme.

Identify and quote specific features of language or structure used by the writers.

Explain how this helps to get across their ideas about the theme.

Connectives

➤ Use connectives of comparison to show the examiner that you are comparing.

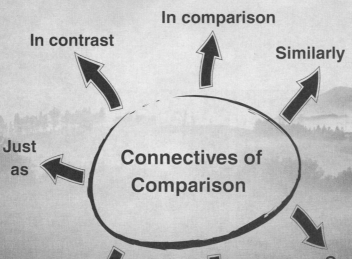

In contrast

In comparison

Similarly

Just as

Connectives of Comparison

On the other hand

Whereas

However

Autobiography ➤ a text written by someone about their own life (whereas a biography is written about someone else's life).

Simile ➤ a descriptive comparison, using like or as.

Metaphor ➤ a descriptive comparison that claims to be true, rather than like or as.

Tone ➤ the emotion in a piece of writing or speech.

🎧 4

Coming Up With Ideas

➤ Look at these extracts of modern non-fiction, focussed on mothers. The first is from an **autobiography**, the second is from a speech at an awards ceremony. A student has underlined features of language and structure that stood out to them.

My mother is scraping a piece of burned toast out of the kitchen window, a crease of annoyance across her forehead. This is not an occasional occurrence, a once-in-awhile hiccup in a busy mother's day. My mother burns the toast as surely as the sun rises each morning. In fact, I doubt if she has ever made a round of toast in her life that failed to fill the kitchen with plumes of throat-catching smoke. I am nine now and have never seen butter without black bits in it.

It is impossible not to love someone who makes toast for you. People's failings, even major ones such as when they make you wear short trousers to school, fall into insignificance as your teeth break through the rough, toasted crust and sink into the doughy cushion of white bread underneath.

(from 'Toast' by Nigel Slater)

And last, my mom. I don't think you know what you did. You had my brother when you were 18 years old. Three years later, I came out. The odds were stacked against us. Single parent with two boys by the time you were 21 years old. Everybody told us we weren't supposed to be here. We went from apartment to apartment by ourselves. One of the best memories I had was when we moved into our first apartment, no bed, no furniture and we just sat in the living room and just hugged each other.

You made us believe. You kept us off the street. You put clothes on our backs, food on the table. When you didn't eat, you made sure we ate. You went to sleep hungry. You sacrificed for us.

(speech by Kevin Durant on collecting the NBA's Most Valuable Player Award in 2014)

➤ If you were comparing how these two authors feel about their mothers, you might get some of these ideas. (You could practise writing some up using the simple comparison structure covered on page 10):

- Both love their mums – emphasised by short sentences.
- Slater seems less close to his mum than Durant – mother / mom.
- Neither mum had a perfect life. One was annoyed by her inability to cook, the other struggled to support her family – use of **metaphor** (and **simile** in the first extract).
- Both mums did their best for their boys – shown through list form and powerful verbs.
- Both have happy memories of their mothers – description of toast / hugging in apartment.
- Slater makes fun of his mum a bit, whilst Durant seems in awe of his mum – use of humour / more serious **tone**, repetition, and powerful verbs.

Find two different texts that have a shared theme. Using a different colour pen for each of your ideas, circle similarities and differences in how the texts approach their theme. To develop this skill, list the different features of language and structure used to get across each writer's idea.

Why do you need to read the question carefully?

What three things should you include in order to structure your comparisons?

List three connectives of comparison.

Things to Remember

➤ In your exam you will be asked to compare a modern text with a 19th century text.

➤ Make sure you read the question carefully, then start looking for points of comparison.

➤ Don't be put off by the fact that 19th century texts can seem more difficult due to longer sentences, more formal writing and more complex or old-fashioned language.

Exploring Language and Structure

➤ Look at these extracts of non-fiction. You have already read the first one from Nigel Slater's autobiography 'Toast'. The second is an extract from the diaries of Charles Darwin, who travelled the world and developed the theory of evolution. How do the two writers show their attitudes towards food?

My mother is scraping a piece of burned toast out of the kitchen window, a crease of annoyance across her forehead. This is not an occasional occurrence, a once-in-a while hiccup in a busy mother's day. My mother burns the toast as surely as the sun rises each morning. In fact, I doubt if she has ever made a round of toast in her life that failed to fill the kitchen with plumes of throat-catching smoke. I am nine now and have never seen butter without black bits in it.

It is impossible not to love someone who makes toast for you. People's failings, even major ones such as when they make you wear short trousers to school, fall into insignificance as your teeth break through the rough, toasted crust and sink into the doughy cushion of white bread underneath.

(from 'Toast' by Nigel Slater)

September 16th.

...We did not reach the posta on the Rio Tapalguen till after it was dark. At supper, from something which was said, I was suddenly struck with horror at thinking that I was eating one of the favourite dishes of the country, namely, a half formed calf, long before its proper time of birth. It turned out to be Puma; the meat is very white, and remarkably like veal in taste. Dr. Shaw was laughed at for stating that "the flesh of the lion is in great esteem, having no small affinity with veal, both in colour, taste, and flavour." Such certainly is the case with the Puma. The Gauchos* differ in their opinion whether the Jaguar is good eating, but are unanimous in saying that cat is excellent.

*Gauchos = a group of people native to the South Americas

(from Charles Darwin's diary, 'The Voyage of the Beagle', 1860)

Possible Ideas

➤ Both describe liking certain foods: adjectives and metaphor to describe toast; adverb and simile to describe puma.

➤ Both show dislike towards food: adjectives and **personification** linked to burned toast; adverb and metaphor when Darwin thinks he's eating something horrible.

➤ Both writers use food to tell the reader about someone: metaphor, simile, short sentence and humour to show his feelings towards his mother; more formal but unusual references to show us how the Gauchos live.

Writing Your Response

➤ Read the start of a student's response, comparing the attitudes towards food that are shown in the two texts. Notice the way the analysis is structured:

In the two extracts, both Slater and Darwin describe their enjoyment of certain foods. Slater describes eating toast, "rough, toasted crust and sink into the doughy cushion". The adjectives and metaphor describe the contrasting textures of the toast and help us to imagine his pleasure. In comparison, Darwin uses a simple simile to help us imagine the taste of a puma, "remarkably like veal in taste". He adds the adverb to show his surprise at enjoying such an unusual meat.

As well as this, both authors show their dislike of certain foods...

Personification ➤ describing a thing as if it has human qualities.

5

clear idea/point of comparison in the first sentence

evidence and analysis of one text

a connective of comparison

evidence and analysis of the other text

a linking connective to introduce your next idea/point of comparison

To help you revise the way to compare a text, turn the flow diagram into a mobile that you can hang up. To develop your skills, find two non-fiction texts, annotate them, and then try to analyse them following the structure on your mobile.

What differences might you notice between modern and 19th century writing?

What do you need to include when comparing modern and 19th century texts?

In what ways do you think a diary is similar and different to an autobiography?

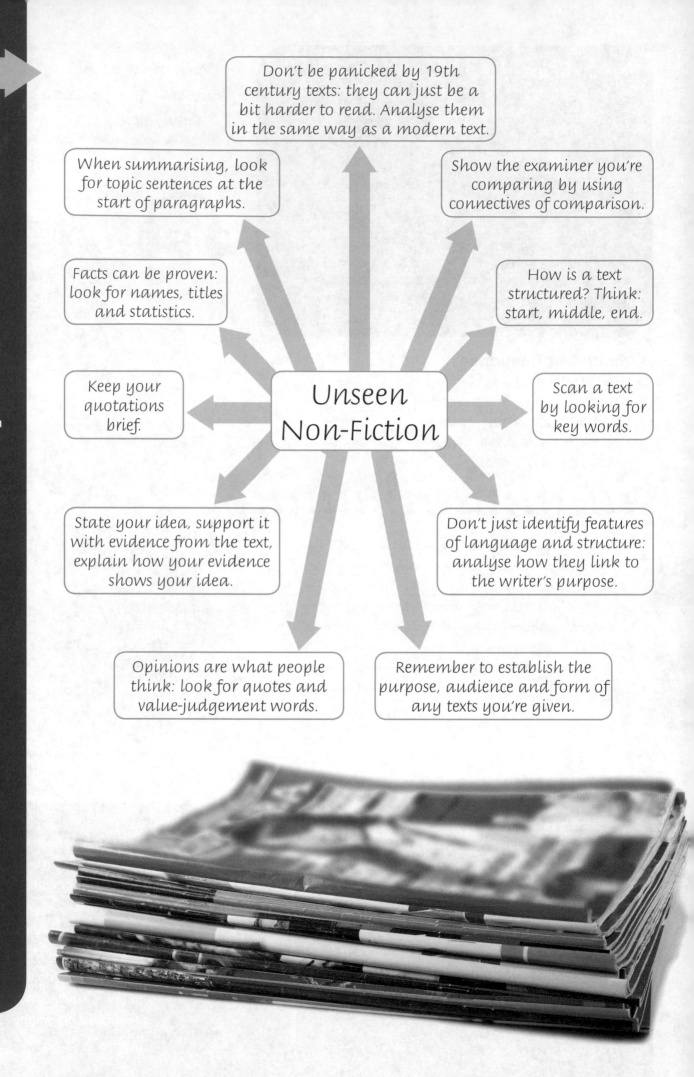

Don't be panicked by 19th century texts: they can just be a bit harder to read. Analyse them in the same way as a modern text.

When summarising, look for topic sentences at the start of paragraphs.

Show the examiner you're comparing by using connectives of comparison.

Facts can be proven: look for names, titles and statistics.

How is a text structured? Think: start, middle, end.

Keep your quotations brief.

Unseen Non-Fiction

Scan a text by looking for key words.

State your idea, support it with evidence from the text, explain how your evidence shows your idea.

Don't just identify features of language and structure: analyse how they link to the writer's purpose.

Opinions are what people think: look for quotes and value-judgement words.

Remember to establish the purpose, audience and form of any texts you're given.

Source A

In this extract from his autobiography, Morrissey describes his school days in 1960s Manchester.

The school looms tall and merciless in central Hulme, as the last of the old order, a giant black shadow of ancient morality since 1842, invoking deliberate apprehension into every wide-eyed small face that cautiously holds back the tears as he or she is left at its steps – into long echoing halls of whitewashed walls, of carbolic and plimsoll and crayon blazing through the senses, demanding that all cheerful thought must now die away. This bleak mausoleum called St Wilfrid's has the power to make you unhappy, and this is the only message it is prepared to give. Padlocks and keys and endless stone stairways, down unlit hallways to darkened cloakrooms where something terrible might befall you.

Children tumble in soaked by rain, and thus they remain for the rest of the day – wet shoes and wet clothes moisten the air, for this is the way. Our teachers, too, are dumped, as we are, in St Wilfrid's parish. There is no money to be had and there are no resources, just as there is no colour and no laughter. These children are slackly shaped and contaminated. Many stragglers stink, and will faint due to lack of food, but there is no such thing as patient wisdom to be found in the sharp agony of the teachers.

Headmaster Mr Coleman rumbles with grumpiness in a rambling stew of hate. He is martyred by his position and is ruled by his apparent loathing of the children. Convincingly old, he is unable to praise, and his military servitude is the murdered child within. His staff stutters on, minus any understanding of the child mind. These educators educate no one, and outside of their occupations they surely lament their own allotted spot? No schoolteacher at St Wilfrid's will smile, and there is no joy to be found between the volcano of resentment offered by Mother Peter, a bearded nun who beats children from dawn to dusk, or Mr Callaghan, the youngest of the crew, eaten up by a resentment that he couldn't control.

The following text is taken from a newspaper article, published in 'The Ashton Weekly Recorder' in 1869.

THE VILLAGE SCHOOL

'Yes, 'tis the old schoolroom. I know it again
Though now it seems smaller, much smaller than then;
But years have rolled on since I stood here before:
And thankful I feel to behold it once more.'

So this the place to which, in years long gone. I was introduced by my elder brother, and placed upon the lowest form. [...] And that is the very peg on which I first hung my rustic cap. There, too, is the desk at which I sat in after years. Here was the stage erected, when, at Christmas tide, we enacted the juvenile drama of Alfred the Great and Gubba, the Saxon farmer, was personated[1] by me, then a farmer's son, and destined to become a farmer myself. How different, however, has been my lot; the dark offices, the dim courts and alleys of the town have been, unwillingly, exchanged for the flowery meads[2] and bright green hedges and fields of my native home. But to return. That is the large door through which we scampered, heels over head, and made the welkin[3] resound with our joyful shouts when an unexpected holiday was proclaimed. That is the old dominie's[4] desk, and fancy portrays the venerable man still presiding there, with that well-worn cane. And there hung the "dunce cap," long disused, but preserved as a relic of the past, and memorial of the penance imposed upon our fathers, when laggard[5] steps brought them late to school. And some of these forms are those which willing hands used to clear, when, at holiday times, that dear old master used to close his eyes, and scatter amongst us the toys and nondescript articles which, having been taken out of their pockets for barter or examination by the lads when in school, had been forfeited by the rules of the school. Those scrambles for the proceeds of the 'forfeit drawer' are never to be forgotten. But how small everything now appears. In my mind's eye and loving memory I had magnified them many times over. What changes few short years have wrought.

1 personated – impersonated, played.
2 meads – meadows
3 welkin – sky
4 dominie – teacher
5 laggard – slow

1. Read Source A.

Choose four statements below which are TRUE.

- Shade the boxes of the ones that you think are true.
- Choose a maximum of four statements.

    A   The school is in Hulme. ☐

    B   The school is over a hundred years old. ☐

    C   The corridors are light and airy. ☐

    D   The children's clothes and shoes are dried when they get in. ☐

    E   The pupils are always laughing. ☐

    F   Some of the children smell unpleasant. ☐

    G   St Wilfrid's is a rich parish. ☐

    H   The headmaster does not understand children. ☐

[4 marks]

2. You need to refer to both Source A and Source B for this question.
Use details from both sources. Write a summary of the similarities
and differences between St. Wilfrid's and the village school.   **[8 marks]**

3. You now need to refer only to Source B, the description of the village school.
How does the writer use language to convey his experience of school?

[8 marks]

4. For this question you need to refer to both Source A and Source B.
Compare how the writers convey different attitudes to their schools.
In your answer you should:
- Compare the different attitudes
- Compare the methods they use to convey these attitudes
- Support your ideas with quotations from both texts   **[16 marks]**

Read the Question

➤ This might seem obvious but you need to make sure you know what you're specifically focussing on, so that all the information you retrieve is relevant.

➤ Examiners can sometimes state where in the text they want you to look: a certain paragraph or specific lines. You won't get marks if you find relevant information but it's from the wrong place.

Synonyms ➤

different words that have the same, or similar, meaning (such as: cold, chilly, freezing).

Facts and Themes

➤ You could be asked to retrieve facts from a text, such as key information about a character, or you could be asked to retrieve information on a theme, like details about the weather.

➤ To help you do this, you need to practise scanning a text: looking quickly through a text to spot relevant words, then reading the surrounding sentences in order to clarify the information.

➤ For facts, look for capital letters (this could indicate names of people or places) and numbers (this could tell you dates or ages).

➤ For themes, look for the actual word (such as nature) but also **synonyms** and related words (like countryside, wildlife, etc.).

> Read the text below.

Margaret was struck afresh by her cousin's beauty. They had grown up together from childhood, and all along Edith had been remarked upon by every one, except Margaret, for her prettiness; but Margaret had never thought about it until the last few days, when the prospect of soon losing her companion seemed to give force to every sweet quality and charm which Edith possessed. They had been talking about wedding dresses, and wedding ceremonies; and Captain Lennox, and what he had told Edith about her future life at Corfu, where his regiment was stationed; and the difficulty of keeping a piano in good tune (a difficulty which Edith seemed to consider as one of the most formidable that could befal her in her married life), and what gowns she should want in the visits to Scotland, which would immediately succeed her marriage; but the whispered tone had latterly become more drowsy; and Margaret, after a pause of a few minutes, found, as she fancied, that in spite of the buzz in the next room, Edith had rolled herself up into a soft ball of muslin and ribbon, and silken curls, and gone off into a peaceful little after-dinner nap.

(from 'North and South' by Elizabeth Gaskell)

> Scan the text to find four facts about Edith, then find four things that Margaret feels about Edith.
> If you looked for capital letters and numbers, you may have found the following facts: Edith's cousin is called Margaret; Edith is going to be marrying Captain Lennox; Edith will be moving to Corfu; Edith will be going to Scotland after her wedding.
> If you looked for the word 'Edith' and any adjectives, you may have found the following opinions: Margaret thinks Edith is beautiful; she doesn't want to be parted from her; Edith is sweet and charming; she is innocent (not aware of the difficulties of marriage/how she looks asleep).

Working with a friend, challenge each other to find specific information. Get an extract of fiction (the opening of any novel will do), read it yourself, and decide on either a theme of information or a set of facts that your friend has to find. You could use highlighters to help you when scanning. To develop your skills, time each other so you get quicker for the actual exam.

1. Why do you need to read the question carefully?
2. What can help you find facts in a text?
3. How can synonyms help you when scanning a text?

When analysing fiction, you should try to comment on how the writer has used sentence structure to convey meaning. For example:

> short sentences for shock or emphasis
> lists to build up ideas
> dashes or **ellipses** to create dramatic pauses
> long sentences to convey a lot of detail
> exclamations or questions to suggest what a character is feeling.

Narrative Structure

> You may also be asked to explore how an extract of fiction is structured. This means what the author has done to establish and develop their writing. Try to think of the extract in terms of its start, middle, and end. For example:

> How does it begin? Do we get characters, setting, events, or a combination of these?
> How does this beginning try to engage the reader?
> What happens in the middle and how does this build on the opening?
> As the extract progresses, does the reader get answers to certain questions or just more questions?
> How does the end of the extract engage the reader?

7

Ellipsis ➤
... used to miss out information.
Suspense ➤
a feeling of exciting uncertainty.

Module 7 | Structure and Development

In the first part of ROBINSON CRUSOE, at page one hundred and twenty-nine, you will find it thus written: — **Suggests something bad may happen**

"Now I saw, though too late, the Folly of beginning a Work before we count the Cost, and before we judge rightly of our own Strength to go through with it."

Short sentence to emphasise suspense — Only yesterday, I opened my ROBINSON CRUSOE at that place. Only this morning (May twenty-first, Eighteen hundred and fifty), came my lady's nephew, Mr. Franklin Blake, and held a short conversation with me, as follows:— **Gradually establishes narrator: well-read, servant, respectful**

Long sentence to add detail and establish plot — "Betteredge," says Mr. Franklin, "I have been to the lawyer's about some family matters; and, among other things, we have been talking of the loss of the Indian Diamond, in my aunt's house in Yorkshire, two years since. /.../ **Establishes date and character / makes it seem more 'real'**

Dash creates a dramatic pause to emphasise the idea that people have suffered — "In this matter of the Diamond," he said, "the characters of innocent people have suffered under suspicion already—as you know. The memories of innocent people may suffer, hereafter, for want of a record of the facts to which those who come after us can appeal. There can be no doubt that this strange family story of ours ought to be told. And I think, Betteredge, Mr. Bruff and I together have hit on the right way of telling it."

Introduces a crime but keeps information brief so the reader wants more

The crime is developed, but still raising questions, through idea of suffering

Very satisfactory to both of them, no doubt. But I failed to see what I myself had to do with it, so far.

Last paragraph establishes how the story will be written (different people's experiences) — "We have certain events to relate," Mr. Franklin proceeded; "and we have certain persons concerned in those events who are capable of relating them. Starting from these plain facts, the idea is that we should all write the story of the Moonstone in turn—as far as our own personal experience extends, and no farther. We must begin by showing how the Diamond first fell into the hands of my uncle Herncastle, when he was serving in India fifty years since. This prefatory narrative I have already got by me in the form of an old family paper, which relates the necessary particulars on the authority of an eye-witness. The next thing to do is to tell how the Diamond found its way into my aunt's house in Yorkshire, two years ago, and how it came to be lost in little more than twelve hours afterwards. Nobody knows as much as you do, Betteredge, about what went on in the house at that time. So you must take the pen in hand, and start the story."

Long sentences to build up our understanding of the plot

We're told more about the story of the diamond, getting the reader more intrigued

Short sentence to create a dramatic way into the story

Betteredge is now going to begin the story; this makes us read on

(from 'The Moonstone' by Wilkie Collins)

Pick the opening page of any novel and turn it into a poster flow diagram of how it engages the reader. Use different colours for start, middle, and end. Pick out key quotations and say how they help to establish and develop the opening. To develop your skills, use another colour to comment on the effects of any particular sentence structures in your quotations.

1. What is the difference between sentence structure and narrative structure?

2. What sort of features of sentence structure should you look out for?

3. How can you split an extract into three to help you consider how it develops?

Language

➤ When the examiner asks you to analyse language, you need to look at the type of words an author uses and how these have an effect on the reader.

➤ You need to say <u>what</u> the author does, support this with a key quotation, and then analyse <u>how</u> this conveys meaning.

Mood

➤ You could be asked to analyse how mood is created by a writer. This means the atmosphere or emotion in the text, such as sad, scary, or calm.

➤ In the extract below, the mood could be described as desperately bored. An examiner could ask you how this is achieved by the author.

The world is full of little towns that people want to leave, and scarcely know why. The hills crowd in too closely, they say, or the plains which stretch around are too featureless, or the freeway runs through, or doesn't run through: you can hardly put your finger on the source of their discontent, or indeed your own. A kind of sorrow creeps along the streets and drags you down; you can hardly lift your feet to shake it off. The shops in the High Street are forever closed for lunch, or would be better if they were: the houses in the centre may be old, veritable antiquities, but still lack resonance: a tuning fork that declines to twang, dead in the face of all expectation. And if nothing happens you know you'll soon be dead as well, or your soul will be.

(from 'Growing Rich' by Fay Weldon)

➤ You could start by picking out the phrases that link to boredom or desperation. For example: 'A kind of sorrow creeps along the streets and drags you down'.

➤ Then identify any language features in your phrases. For instance, the quotation above uses **personification** and powerful verbs.

➤ Then think about how that creates a mood of desperate boredom. For example, the personification makes the whole town seem miserable and dull (added to by the slow verb 'creep'), but also that this mood of boredom is oppressive and gets to everyone (the verb phrase 'drags you down').

What else could you add about how the extract creates a mood of desperate boredom?

Character and Setting
➤ You could be asked to analyse how an author presents a character and/or setting.
➤ In the extract below the character could be described as old and creepy.

We should not have seen so much but for a lighted lantern that an old man in spectacles and a hairy cap was carrying about in the shop. Turning towards the door, he now caught sight of us. He was short, cadaverous, and withered, with his head sunk sideways between his shoulders and the breath issuing in visible smoke from his mouth as if he were on fire within. His throat, chin, and eyebrows were so frosted with white hairs and so gnarled with veins and puckered skin that he looked from his breast upward like some old root in a fall of snow.

(from 'Bleak House' by Charles Dickens)

➤ If you were focussing on character, you could start by picking out the phrases that describe the character's age or make him sound creepy. For example: 'short, cadaverous, and withered'.
➤ Identify any language features. For instance, the quotation above uses a pattern of three powerful adjectives.
➤ Think about how that makes the man seem old or creepy. For example, the pattern of three adjectives highlights the immediate impression the old man has on the narrator. 'Withered' suggests he is very wrinkled and looked as if he is dying. This is emphasised by 'cadaverous', which means he looks like a dead body.
➤ What else could you add about how the extract creates character or setting?

Personification ➤
describing an object or thing as
if it has human qualities.

'Explode' a text. Choose the opening page of any novel. Photocopy it, then cut up all the key phrases and stick them to a sheet of A3 under the headings: mood, character, setting.
To develop your skills, use different colours to highlight and analyse the effects of different language features.

1. What three areas of an unseen fiction text might you be asked to analyse in terms of language?
2. How will WHAT and HOW help you to analyse language?
3. What sort of features of language might you look out for?

Use a simple analysis structure: state a point > support it with evidence > analyse how features of language or structure in your quotation get across the point you made.

Features of language = verb, adjective, adverb, pronoun, simile, metaphor, personification, contrast, etc.

Unseen Fiction

Use key words and synonyms to find ideas on a theme

Sentence structure = lists, short sentences, long sentences, exclamations, questions, dashes, etc.

Scan the text to find information.

Use capital letters and numbers to find facts

Narrative structure = start, middle, and end

How does an extract establish characters, settings and themes?

How does an extract develop as it goes on?

> **Read this opening of the novel 'The Collector' by John Fowles. It is about a man who collects butterflies, but he becomes obsessed with a girl called Miranda.**

WHEN she was home from her boarding-school I used to see her almost every day sometimes, because their house was right opposite the Town Hall Annexe. She and her younger sister used to go in and out a lot, often with young men, which of course I didn't like. When I had a free moment from the files and ledgers I stood by the window and used to look down over the road over the frosting and sometimes I'd see her. In the evening I marked it in my observations diary, at first with X, and then when I knew her name with M. I saw her several times outside too. I stood right behind her once in a queue at the public library down Crossfield Street. She didn't look once at me, but I watched the back of her head and her hair in a long pigtail. It was very pale, silky, like burnet cocoons. All in one pigtail coming down almost to her waist, sometimes in front, sometimes at the back. Sometimes she wore it up. Only once, before she came to be my guest here, did I have the privilege to see her with it loose, and it took my breath away it was so beautiful, like a mermaid.

Another time one Saturday off when I went up to the Natural History Museum I came back on the same train. She sat three seats down and sideways to me, and read a book, so I could watch her for thirty-five minutes. Seeing her always made me feel like I was catching a rarity, going up to it very careful, heart-in-mouth as they say. A Pale Clouded Yellow, for instance. I always thought of her like that, I mean words like elusive and sporadic, and very refined – not like the other ones, even the pretty ones. More for the real connoisseur.

Well, then there was the bit in the local paper about the scholarship she'd won and how clever she was, and her name as beautiful as herself, Miranda. So I knew she was up in London studying art. It really made a difference, that newspaper article. It seemed like we became more intimate, although of course we still did not know each other in the ordinary way.

elusive = difficult to find or catch   *connoisseur = an expert*

1. Find four facts about Miranda from paragraph 1.   **[4 marks]**

2. How has the writer structured the text in order to engage the reader?   **[8 marks]**

3. How does Fowles use language to show the speaker's obsession with Miranda?   **[8 marks]**

4. How far do you agree that the speaker comes across as frightening rather than romantic?   **[20 marks]**

The Basics

➤ You might be expected to describe something completely imaginary (such as a futuristic world) or a particular scene (for example, a happy memory).

➤ Develop your descriptions so the reader can really imagine what you're writing about.

➤ Try to establish settings (and character if necessary) and create a powerful atmosphere.

➤ Avoid obvious descriptive choices and be creative.

➤ Try not to keep using general verbs (such as look, go, say); instead, use more specific alternatives (like glance, rush, whisper).

➤ Remember connectives of time and place so your writing is structured clearly.

➤ Don't get carried away by your description and forget about your written accuracy.

Descriptive Techniques

➤ Use a range of descriptive techniques so that your writing is interesting and varied. The reader needs to be able to picture your ideas clearly, but should also find what you've written interesting and original.

Senses (sight, smell, sound, touch, taste)

Interesting verbs (doing words), adjectives (describing words) and adverbs (words that describe verbs)

Simile (a comparison using like or as)

Sibilance (a series of words containing s sounds)

Descriptive Techniques

Metaphor (an impossible comparison that claims to be true)

Alliteration (a series of words beginning with the same sound)

Onomatopoeia (words that sound like the word they refer to)

Personification (giving nouns human characteristics)

Sentence Structures

➤ Try to use different sentence structures to create specific effects. For example:

Short, simple sentences	Compound sentences	Complex sentences	Lists
To surprise the reader: *The girl had vanished.*	To create a contrast: *His heart was pounding but his face looked calm.*	To add extra detail: *The rain poured down, hitting the windows like bullets.*	To build up a powerful image: *The gale force winds snapped branches from trees, ripped tiles from roofs, overturned cars and pulled down pylons.*

1. Using the senses

Sight – long corridors, every seat taken inside, changing views from window

Sound – crackling announcements, chatter of passengers

Touch – squeezing past people in carriage

Task: Describe a train journey

Taste – tea, chocolate, cheese sandwich

Smell – damp clothes, perfume

2. Big to Small

Task: Describe your school

1. Bird's eye view – shaped like a ship jutting into the road

2. New purple brick, wooden facing

3. Narrow corridor – walls half-glazed so identical classroom can be seen

4. Newly painted room, cheerful displays in too-small room

5. Six grumpy pupils sitting on plastic seats huddled round plastic tables joined together

---

Make a descriptive writing dice. Print off a cube template from the internet and write different descriptive techniques on each side. Working in a pair, challenge each other to describe something. For each sentence you write, roll the dice and make sure you include the technique that has been rolled. To develop your skills, make another dice that includes the four sentence structures, plus an exclamation mark and an ellipsis; roll both dice together and try to write the technique using the given sentence type or punctuation.

1. When you are writing to describe, what are you trying to give to the reader?
2. What different techniques can you use to build up your descriptions?
3. What effects can you achieve by using different sentence structures?

The Basics

➤ A **narrative** is an account of events – real or imagined.
➤ Paper 1 of the exam is likely to include a task which asks you to write a story or part of a story (probably the beginning).
➤ You will be given a **stimulus** for your story. This could be a picture or a brief instruction. The instructions might tell you what your audience is – usually people of your own age.

10

Genre ➤
a style of literature.

Narrative ➤
a story or account of events.

Stimulus ➤
something to help you get started with your story.

Protagonist ➤
the main character.

Chronological ➤
putting events in the order in which they happen.

Direct speech ➤
the words spoken by a character, indicated by speech marks.

Key Features of Writing to Narrate

➤ Narratives are usually written in the past tense but present tense narratives can be effective in making the action vivid.
➤ You can write using either the first or the third person. Make sure that you are consistent.
➤ Focus on your **protagonist** and think carefully about what he or she is like. The protagonist can be you or a made-up character.
➤ Narratives are usually written in Standard English. However, in a first person narrative you should think about your protagonist's voice, i.e. how he or she would speak.
➤ You can use **direct speech** but do not overdo it. Only use it when it is necessary for the story.
➤ Use descriptive language to create mood and atmosphere.

Plan and Structure Your Answer

➤ Narratives are normally in **chronological** order but you might want to include 'flashbacks' to include events that occurred before the main action.
➤ If you are writing only the beginning of a story, make sure that you understand where the story is going.
➤ If you are writing a complete story, do a quick plan so that your story has a clear beginning, middle and end.

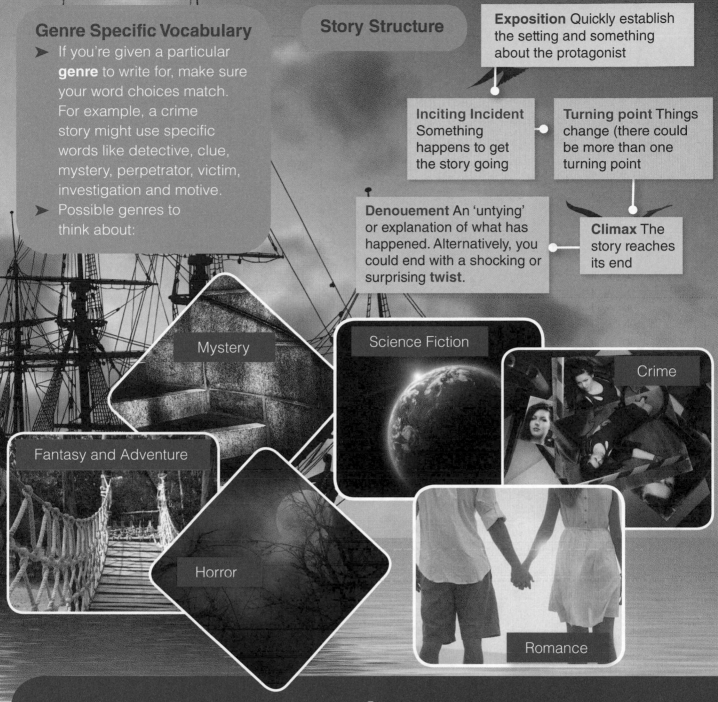

Genre Specific Vocabulary

➤ If you're given a particular **genre** to write for, make sure your word choices match. For example, a crime story might use specific words like detective, clue, mystery, perpetrator, victim, investigation and motive.

➤ Possible genres to think about:

Story Structure

Exposition Quickly establish the setting and something about the protagonist

Inciting Incident Something happens to get the story going

Turning point Things change (there could be more than one turning point)

Denouement An 'untying' or explanation of what has happened. Alternatively, you could end with a shocking or surprising **twist**.

Climax The story reaches its end

Mystery

Science Fiction

Crime

Fantasy and Adventure

Horror

Romance

Try keeping a diary for a week. Write down everything interesting that happens. At the end of the week pick out the most important events and use them to make a plan for a piece of narrative writing. Decide who are the main characters (apart from you). Add brief descriptions of people and places. Then write a first person narrative. Then imagine that you are not involved in the story, but seeing it from the outside, and re-write it as a third person narrative.

1. What is a narrative and who is a narrator?
2. What might flashbacks tell you about?
3. What is a protagonist?

The Basics

➤ In your exam (English Language Paper 2) you will be given a statement and asked to give your view on it.

➤ You may agree or disagree with the statement but it is important that you present both sides of the issue in a **balanced argument** before making clear which side you are on.

➤ Use **topic sentences** at the start of your paragraph to help the audience follow your argument.

➤ Structure your ideas clearly in order to present your argument fully. For example:

Using a short, introductory paragraph, state the issue being debated.

Write a series of paragraphs arguing why you are for or against the issue. Make your views varied and offer clear reasons or evidence.

Then include several paragraphs looking at the alternative views. For each one, unless it has been covered already, offer your counter-argument.

In your final paragraph, present your conclusion and summarise why you are for or against the issue.

Making Use of Persuasive Techniques

➤ In order to make your argument more effective, use some of the FORESTRY techniques (see page 32). But don't forget that you're giving both sides of the argument not just your favoured viewpoint:

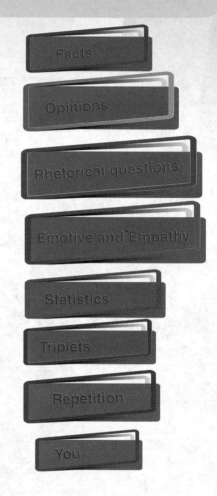

Facts
Opinions
Rhetorical questions
Emotive and Empathy
Statistics
Triplets
Repetition
You

Balanced argument ➤

presenting both sides of an issue, not just your personal view.

Topic sentence ➤

a sentence that opens a paragraph by indicating what it will be about.

Conclusion ➤

Drawing together different viewpoints and ideas before making a final judgement.

Connectives

➤ You'll need to use lots of different connectives in order to help your audience follow your argument clearly.

➤ Connectives of comparison should be used to build up your argument, whilst connectives of contrast should be used to present the alternative view and any counter-arguments. As well as this, you should use connectives of cause and effect in order to explain why you think what you do.

Connectives of		
Comparison	Contrast	Cause and Effect
In comparison	In contrast	As a result
Similarly	On the other hand	Because of this
Furthermore	However	Therefore
Just as	While	Consequently

➤ You'll also need to use connectives at the end of your writing to signal to the audience that you're bringing your argument to its **conclusion**. For example: In conclusion, To summarise, Overall.

Make a list of issues or debates that interest you, such as building new facilities for young people, shortening the school holidays, making everyone stay in education until the age of 18. Then create balanced argument posters. Put the points for the issue on the left hand side, and the points against the issue down the right hand side. In the centre, draw two images that summarise the main arguments. To develop your skills, try to put contrasting points opposite each other or add in counter-arguments in a different coloured pen.

1. What two purposes does writing a point of view have?

2. What should you include in your final paragraph?

3. What different connectives will you need to use?

The Basics

➤ When you argue your point of view, you are trying to **persuade** your reader to agree with you.

➤ Make sure you know who you're persuading. The question might specify an audience, e.g. young people or the school governors.

➤ Make sure you know what form you are writing in, e.g. an article for a newspaper or magazine.

Persuade ➤

get someone to think or behave in a certain way.

Mnemonic ➤

something that helps with memory.

Persuasive Techniques

➤ Revise different persuasive techniques, using the **mnemonic** FORESTRY:

Facts: Support your argument with lots of facts, so you sound like you know what you're talking about.

Opinions: Get your views across in a powerful way; state your opinions as if they are actual facts, rather than writing uncertain phrases like 'I think' or 'maybe'.

Rhetorical questions: These are questions that you ask to get your audience thinking. For example, What can you do to protect the environment?

Emotive and Empathy: Use emotive language to make your readers feel something, such as pride, sympathy or guilt. Empathise with their feelings: by acknowledging their concerns, you can try to win them round.

Statistics: Like using facts, include statistics to make your persuasive points sound researched. This is a test of your writing (not your statistical knowledge) so, as long as they sound realistic, you can make them up.

Triplets: Organise ideas and examples into patterns of three, or triplets, to emphasise a point.

Repetition: Repeat words or phrases in order to highlight a point.

You: When writing to persuade it's much more effective if you address your audience directly ('you', also known as the second person).

Structuring Your Ideas

➤ Start a new paragraph for each of your persuasive points.

➤ Use connectives of sequence to make the different parts of a speech clear to the reader (such as, firstly, next, finally).

➤ Use connectives of comparison to build up your persuasive points (similarly, as well as this, just as).

12

Make persuasive technique cue cards, plus a series of cards with persuasive topics on (such as building a new supermarket, banning homework, or having the next World Cup in England). Working with friends, deal the techniques cards out so everybody has one and then turn over one of the topic cards. Everyone has to come up with a persuasive sentence for the topic, using the technique on their card. If you can't do it, you're out. Keep going round until one person is left; they win that topic card. Then re-deal the techniques cards and turn over a new topic card.

1. As well as your own opinions, what do you need to consider when trying to persuade someone?

2. What mnemonic will help you remember different persuasive techniques?

3. What are the different persuasive techniques in the mnemonic?

Why Spelling is Important

➤ All of your exams will contain a mark for your written accuracy, especially when your writing skills are being tested. If you struggle with your spelling, you should try to improve it by getting in the habit of reading a lot and trying different online tests.

➤ Don't make mistakes spelling words that are already spelled for you on the exam paper.

➤ If time is short before your exams, you could focus on improving the key areas covered on these pages.

Plural ➤
when there is more than one of something

Abbreviation ➤
shortening of words

Preposition ➤
a word to show the position of things in terms of time or place

Subject Specific Words

➤ Make sure you have learned the sort of words that you will use regularly in your English exams. For example:

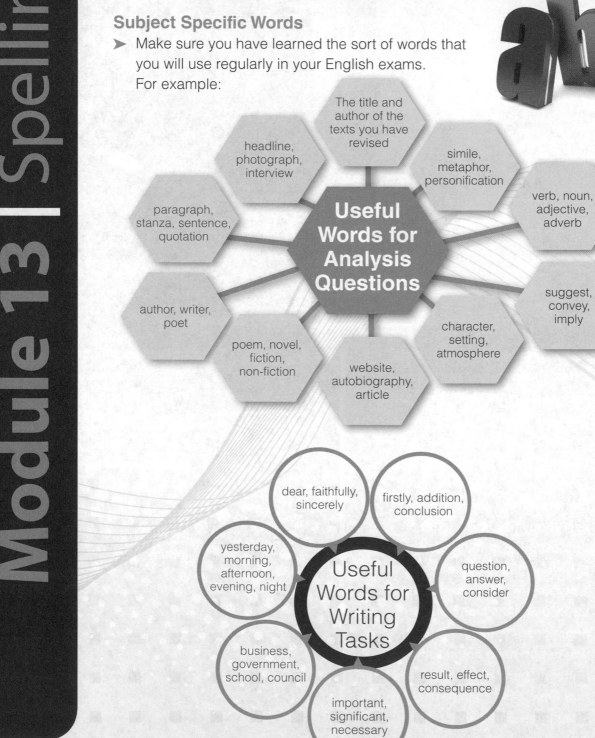

Useful Words for Analysis Questions

- The title and author of the texts you have revised
- headline, photograph, interview
- simile, metaphor, personification
- verb, noun, adjective, adverb
- paragraph, stanza, sentence, quotation
- suggest, convey, imply
- author, writer, poet
- poem, novel, fiction, non-fiction
- website, autobiography, article
- character, setting, atmosphere

Useful Words for Writing Tasks

- dear, faithfully, sincerely
- firstly, addition, conclusion
- yesterday, morning, afternoon, evening, night
- question, answer, consider
- business, government, school, council
- result, effect, consequence
- important, significant, necessary

Homophones
➤ Homophones are words that sound the same but have different meanings and spellings. Try to remember the spellings of key homophones so you don't make silly mistakes.

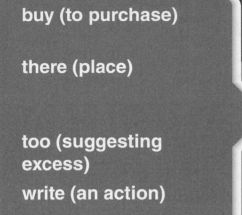

buy (to purchase)

there (place)

too (suggesting excess)

write (an action)

where (place)

your (ownership)

by (a **preposition** meaning near or on)

their (ownership)

two (a number)

right (a direction, or being correct)

wear (to put on)

you're (abbreviation of you are)

bye (**abbreviation** of goodbye)

they're (abbreviation of they are)

to (a preposition of direction)

Word Endings
➤ Students also make mistakes with the endings of words. Over the next few weeks or months, when you're reading, look out for the following things about word endings:

➤ Do nouns end in -s or -es for their **plural**? (car = cars; box = boxes) Nouns ending with a -y become -ies for their plural. (baby = babies)
➤ When verbs change tense, which words just add -ing or -ed, and which words also double the last consonant? (play = playing/played; scan = scanning/scanned)
➤ Which verbs change completely in the past tense? (run = ran; say = said)
➤ Learn familiar word endings that appear a lot. For example: -tion (attention, motion); -ble (able, horrible); -ous (gorgeous, adventurous).

Make a word wheel of subject specific words that you're struggling with. Give it to a friend and ask them to spin it and test you. To develop your skills, play lots of word games in magazines and online, such as 'Scrabble' or 'Words With Friends'.

1. How many words can you list that end -tion?
2. What are the differences in meaning between there, their, and they're?
3. What other homophones do you know and what are their different meanings?

Sentences

➤ You should use a variety of sentence structures in your writing. This will show you have a good level of literacy, as well as bringing variety to your work and allowing you to use sentences to achieve different effects.

➤ In order to structure a range of sentences, you need to understand the three basic types.

➤ Simple sentences contain one verb and one idea (The old house was deserted.)

➤ Compound sentences are two simple sentences joined by a **conjunction** (The old house was deserted and its windows were all broken.)

➤ Complex sentences have a **main clause** and a **subordinate clause**, separated by a comma (The old house was deserted, its smashed windows revealing only darkness within.)

➤ Complex sentences are the main type of sentence you should be using as they allow you to present your ideas in detail. The main clause should always make sense on its own, but the subordinate clause will not make sense on its own.

➤ The subordinate clause can also be put in different positions to add further variety to your writing: before the main clause (Its smashed windows revealing only darkness within, the old house was deserted.); in the middle of the main clause (The old house, its smashed windows revealing only darkness within, was deserted.); after the main clause (The old house was deserted, its smashed windows revealing only darkness within). Notice that you need two commas if you place the subordinate clause in the middle of the main clause.

Tenses

➤ When you're writing, you need to choose a tense that matches your purpose and form. For example, if you're describing something that has happened it needs to be in the past tense, or if you're inviting people to a forthcoming event you would need to use the future tense, but if you're writing about what something is currently like you would use the present tense.

➤ You need to make sure that your tense choices are consistent and correct, otherwise your work will be confusing to read.

Conjunction ➤
a joining word (for example: and, but, whilst).

Main clause ➤
the main idea in a sentence (it should always make sense on its own).

Subordinate clause ➤
additional information in a sentence.

Dialect ➤
words or phrases used in a particular geographical area.

Slang ➤
informal language, often local and changing quickly.

Standard English

➤ Standard English is the version of English widely accepted as being correct.

➤ When writing answers in your exam you should almost always write in Standard English.

➤ You may use non-standard forms of English, for example **dialect** or **slang**, in dialogue or if you are writing a story in the first person and you think the narrator would not use Standard English.

Personal Pronouns

➤ Be careful not to confuse 'I' and 'me'. 'I' is the subject of a sentence and 'me' is the object.

➤ People often say, for example, 'Me and my friend went to town'. You would not say, 'Me went to town'. Whether you went on your own or with a friend, the correct form is 'I' – My friend and I went to town.

➤ Sometimes, trying to be correct people use 'I as the object – ' The teacher gave my friend and I a detention' . You would not say, 'The teacher gave I detention', but 'The teacher gave me a detention'. Therefore, it should be 'The teacher gave my friend and me a detention.'

➤ Remember that the second person (you) is the same whether you are addressing one person (singular) or more than one (plural). If you love one person you say 'I love you'. If you love everyone in your class, you should still say, 'I love you'.

Try recording a conversation between a group of your friends. When you have listened to the recording, transcribe it (write it out). Pick out words and phrases that your friends have used that are not Standard English. Re-write the dialogue using Standard English.

1. What are the three main types of sentence?

2. When might it be acceptable to use non-standard English in an exam?

3. Which tense would you use when writing about something that has already happened?

Punctuation

➤ Correct punctuation is important because it gives order to your writing and helps it to make sense.
➤ You need to be able to use basic punctuation such as full stops, commas, question marks and exclamation marks.
➤ To gain a good grade you need to use a range of punctuation correctly. This might include colons and semi-colons, inverted commas, dashes and **parentheses**.

Ending Sentences

➤ A full stop is the usual way of separating sentences. Beware of using commas instead of full stops.
➤ A question mark can be used in direct speech when someone asks a question. You can also use it for a **rhetorical question**, when you want your reader to think about something (e.g. How much longer do we have to put up with this inefficiency?).
➤ An exclamation mark can be used to show extreme emotion, surprise or shock (e.g. I don't believe it!)

Commas

➤ As well as using commas to separate the main and subordinate clauses in a complex sentence, you should also remember to use commas between items in a list.
➤ You can choose whether your last item has a comma or not as there is no set rule. For example:
  ➤ I bought apples, oranges, pears, and lemons.
  ➤ I bought comic books, sweets, toys and comics.

Other Punctuation Marks

➤ Colons (:) are used:
  – before explanations (e.g. I was very tired: I had been working all day.)
  – to introduce quotations
  – to introduce lists
➤ Semi-colons (;) are used:
  – to separate items in a list if each item consists of a few words (e.g. I had a full shopping bag: a dozen apples; six ripe oranges; a rather bruised pear; and more lemons than I needed.).
  – to show two clauses are closely related when you do not want to use a connective or a full stop (e.g. The apples are red; the pears are green.).
➤ Dashes (-) are used to show an interruption in your train of thought.
➤ Parentheses (brackets) are used to separate short pieces of extra information within a sentence.
➤ Ellipsis (…) is used:
  – to show that a thought is trailing off
  – to make the reader wonder what comes next.

Apostrophes

Abbreviation
Add an apostrophe where two words have been joined and letters missed out (could have > could've; he is > he's).

Single ownership
Just add 's (the dog's bone; Jack's coat).

The Different Uses of Apostrophes

Ownership when the person's name ends with an -s
Still add 's (Jess's bag; Mr Jones's house). However, if their name ends with an -iz sound, just add the apostrophe (Mrs Bridges' car).

When something is owned by a group
Just add the apostrophe (the two dogs' bone; the boys' coats).

Capital Letters

➤ Students often make careless mistakes with capital letters.
➤ You need them at the start of a sentence.
➤ If the letter i is being used as a pronoun it should be capitalised. For example: I, I've, I'd.
➤ You need them for **proper nouns**: the *names* of people, establishments, towns and countries, etc. For example: Mike, West Lodge School, Northampton, Ireland.

Inverted Commas

Inverted commas are also called speech marks and quotation marks, depending on when they are being used:

➤ They are used in direct speech around the actual words spoken: 'Thank you,' she said. 'That was lovely.'
➤ When quoting, put them around any words taken directly from the text: Wordsworth describes the daffodils 'fluttering and dancing in the breeze'.
➤ They are used for titles: 'My Last Duchess' is a dramatic monologue.

Parentheses ➤
brackets

Rhetorical question ➤
a question not requiring an answer

Proper Noun ➤
a noun that has a specific name or title and a capital letter

1. What are the three main uses of inverted commas?
2. When should you use capital letters?
3. What are the two main uses of an apostrophe?

Planning

➤ Once you've read the question and understood your purpose, audience and form, you should plan your response.

➤ Using whatever method you prefer, come up with different ideas for the content of your task.

➤ You could also note any specific techniques that you might use to convey different bits of your content.

Structuring

➤ When you've got your ideas noted down, you should read them through and number them in a logical order.

➤ You can treat each number as a paragraph and this will ensure that your ideas flow sensibly and allow you to build your writing up.

Example of a Student's Plan

4) Give arguments about why it might be a waste of time – what percentage of waste can be recycled — is the effect on the environment exaggerated – use statistics and anecdotes – put counter arguments, e.g. every little helps.

2) Explain problems with environment linked to lack of recycling – too many rubbish dumps, burning rubbish leads to harmful gases in atmosphere. Emotive language about destroying the planet. Rhetorical question.

'Recycling rubbish is a complete waste of time.'
Write an article for a magazine in which you explain your point of view on this statement.

1) Opening with a brief introduction giving initial response to the statement.

5) More arguments why it may be a waste of time – confusion about what can be recycled – frustration with different bins and petty rules – anecdotal evidence and examples of practice – counter arguments, e.g. this is about having more effective recycling not no recycling.

6) Sum up arguments for and against the statement before putting forward own point of view in strong and convincing way.

3) How recycling helps – not using up the world's resources. Statistic about trees being cut down for paper.

Developing

➤ Make sure that each paragraph is fully developed.

➤ Don't just move onto a new paragraph each time you've written an idea. Think about whether you can build on it or emphasise it. For example, this could be done through lots of detailed imagery (in descriptive writing), or by giving examples and evidence to support your ideas, etc.

➤ Developing your work allows you to show off your skills as a writer, giving you the room to use a range of language and sentence structures.

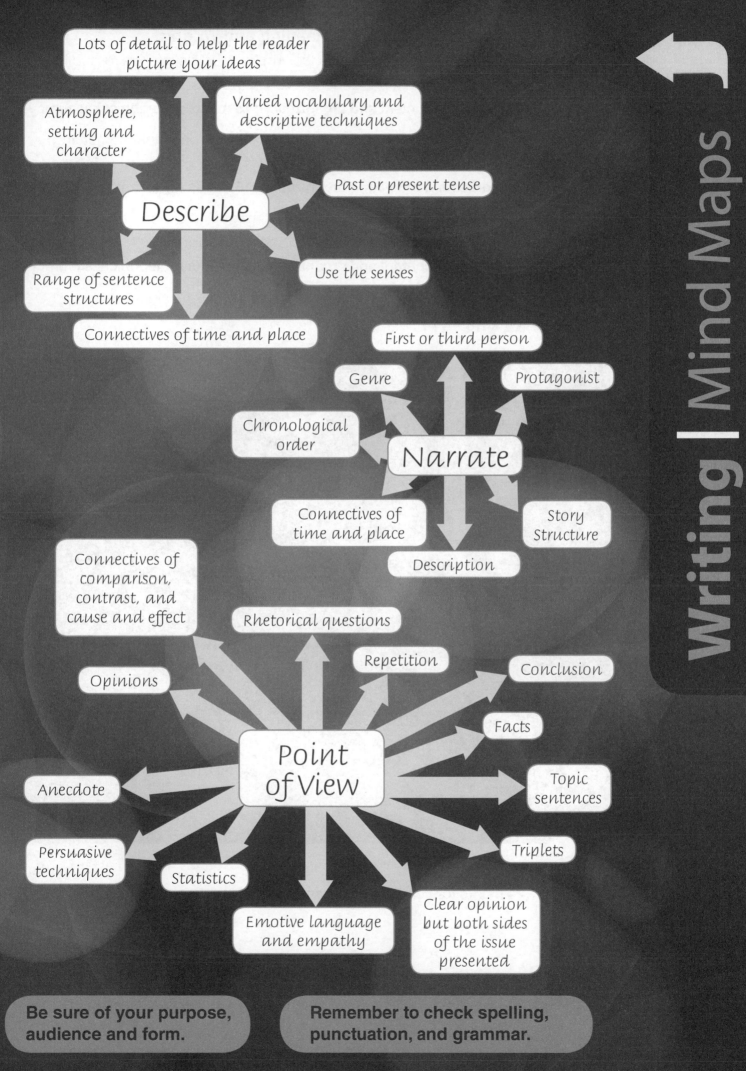

Lots of detail to help the reader picture your ideas

Varied vocabulary and descriptive techniques

Atmosphere, setting and character

Past or present tense

Describe

Use the senses

Range of sentence structures

Connectives of time and place

First or third person

Genre

Protagonist

Chronological order

Narrate

Connectives of time and place

Story Structure

Description

Connectives of comparison, contrast, and cause and effect

Rhetorical questions

Repetition

Conclusion

Opinions

Facts

Anecdote

Point of View

Topic sentences

Triplets

Persuasive techniques

Statistics

Emotive language and empathy

Clear opinion but both sides of the issue presented

Be sure of your purpose, audience and form.

Remember to check spelling, punctuation, and grammar.

Paper 1 – Explorations in Creative Reading and Writing

1. A magazine that you read regularly is looking for 'true life' stories to publish. Write about something that happened to you in the past. **[40 marks]**

    (24 marks for content and organization; 16 marks for technical accuracy)

2. Write the opening of a story that begins: 'She knew at once that something was wrong.' **[40 marks]**

    (24 marks for content and organization; 16 marks for technical accuracy)

3. You have decided to enter a competition in a magazine aimed at people of your own age. Your task is to describe someone you admire. **[40 marks]**

    (24 marks for content and organization; 16 marks for technical accuracy)

4. You are entering a competition in a creative writing magazine. Write a description inspired by this photograph.

[40 marks]

(24 marks for content and organization; 16 marks for technical accuracy)

Paper 2 – Writers' Viewpoints and Perspectives

1. 'School uniforms are old-fashioned and unnecessary. Students are individuals and should have the freedom to express themselves through the way they dress.'

   ➤ Write an article for a magazine in which you express your point of view on this subject. **[40 marks]**

   (24 marks for content and organization; 16 marks for technical accuracy)

2. 'Social media is no longer an innocent amusement. Its misuse has led to all kinds of problems for young people. Sensible parents would ban them from using it altogether.'

   ➤ Write a letter to a broadsheet newspaper expressing your point of view on this subject. **[40 marks]**

   (24 marks for content and organization; 16 marks for technical accuracy)

3. 'There is not enough for young people to do in this area. It is time the council spent some money on providing leisure facilities exclusively for them.'

   ➤ Write an article for your local paper expressing your point of view on this subject. **[40 marks]**

   (24 marks for content and organization; 16 marks for technical accuracy)

4. 'Schooldays are the best days of your life.'

   ➤ Write an article for a broadsheet newspaper in which you express your point of view on this subject. **[40 marks]**

   (24 marks for content and organization; 16 marks for technical accuracy)

Re-reading Poems

You will have studied a selection of poetry from the AQA Anthology in class, either Love and Relationships or Power and Conflict. Make sure you have read the poems several times before going into the exam.

Voice

➤ When re-reading a poem think about the voice – who is speaking.

➤ Many poems are very personal and the poet is 'in' the poem, giving his or her own thoughts and feelings, e.g. Barrett Browning's 'Sonnet 29' or Wilfred Owen's 'Exposure'.

➤ In other poems the poet adopts a '**persona**', creating a character and speaking in his or her voice, e.g. Mew's farmer in 'The Farmer's Bride' or the soldier in Armitage's 'Remains'.

➤ You should also think about who, if anyone, is being addressed.

➤ In the Love and Relationships poems, the poets often speak directly to someone they love or used to love, e.g. Byron's 'When We Two Parted' and Duffy's 'Before You Were Mine'.

➤ In Browning's 'My Last Duchess' the persona speaks to an unnamed person who has been sent to him to discuss a future marriage. In 'The Charge of the Light Brigade' Tennyson addresses the reader at the end of the poem.

Context

➤ You need to show that you are aware of the context of any poem you write about.

➤ This includes an understanding of the time and place in which the poem is set, e.g. the First World War trenches in 'Exposure'.

➤ The poets' attitudes to their subjects should be seen in the context of their time. 'The Charge of the Light Brigade' reflects the views of many who, like Tennyson, had read about the charge in the newspaper. 'Remains' reflects modern concerns about the psychological effect of war on soldiers.

➤ Social issues, such as cultural identity and gender, feature in poems such as 'Checking Out Me History' and 'The Farmer's Bride'.

➤ Context also refers to poetic movements and traditions. Wordsworth, Byron and Shelley were part of the Romantic movement, which valued emotion above intellect and used traditional forms.

Persona ➤
a character adopted by a poet writing in the first person

Enjambment ➤
carrying a sentence across two lines or stanzas of poetry

Pattern of three ➤
three related ideas in a list

Stanza ➤
a section of a poem, sometimes called a verse

Learn Your Techniques

➤ When you look at lines of poetry that get across a poet's ideas, you need to be able to comment on the language and structure that they are using.

➤ Make sure that you know the following language techniques:

Language Techniques	
Adjective	a word that describes a noun or object.
Adverb	a word that describes a verb.
Alliteration	repeating the same sound at the start of a series of words.
Assonance	repeating vowel sounds within a series of words.
Contrast	using two opposite ideas or images.
Metaphor	a comparison that is impossible but is written as if true (rather than 'like').
Onomatopoeia	words that sound like the word they refer to.
Personification	writing about an object or idea as if it has human qualities.
Simile	a comparison that uses 'like' or 'as'.
Symbolism	an image that represents another meaning (e.g. red can symbolise love or danger).
Verb	a word that conveys an action.

➤ You should also learn to identify different features of structure.

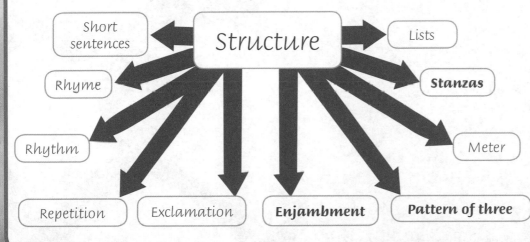

Read your anthology poems out loud to get a sense of how sound relates to meaning. You might want to do this with a partner, taking turns at reading and listening. Look on the internet for recordings of poets reading their own poems. After listening, reflect on whether their readings have changed your feelings about the poems.

1. What are the definitions of verb, adjective, and adverb?
2. What is the difference between a simile and a metaphor?
3. What different structural techniques can a poet use to emphasise ideas?

➤ In your exam you will be given a poem from the Anthology, which you will have to compare with another Anthology poem of your choice.

Grouping Poems Together by Theme

➤ To help you revise, think about the ways in which some of your poems are similar.

➤ For example, if you're studying Love and Relationships, some of the poems might be about romantic love, family relationships, sexual desire, or unrequited love.

➤ Similarly, if you're studying Power and Conflict, you might have themes of personal disagreements, individuals in a war, the effects of war, or the causes of conflict.

➤ Some poems will go into more than one group.

➤ When you've grouped your poems, think about which lines are particularly good at conveying the poets' messages.

Image ➤

a 'word picture' created by the poet which can either be a literal description or a figurative image, such as a metaphor or simile

Attitude ➤

the poet's thoughts or feelings about the subject

Grouping Poems Together by Technique

➤ Another way to revise your poems is to group them by technique.

➤ Which ones use similes in an effective way, or create surprising images, or convey their ideas through metaphor, or use repetition to highlight their viewpoint?

➤ This will give you a deeper understanding of how the poets are using language and structure in their work.

➤ As well as identifying different techniques, you need to think about how they help to get across a poet's ideas. Are they creating a memorable **image**, or helping the reader to imagine something, or highlighting important words, or emphasising a key point, or building up an idea?

Comparing Poems

In your answer you need to compare the two poems'…

➤ themes, ideas and **attitudes**
➤ form and structure
➤ use of language, including imagery.

Approaching the Question

Read the question carefully and read the poem printed on the exam paper.

⬇

Choose the poem you are going to compare it to, thinking about which poems relate to the question and which poems you feel confident about.

⬇

Make a quick plan, briefly noting similarities and differences.

⬇

Explore key points in the first poem.

⬇

Explore key points from the second poem, relating each one back to the first poem.

OR

Explore a key point from both poems, comparing them as you go, e.g. In both 'When We Two Parted' and 'Neutral Tones' the poets directly address people they once loved'.

⬇

Continue to do this throughout your answer.

⬇

Concluding paragraph.
Refer to the question and summarise your main ideas.

On a sheet of A3 paper, make a table that explores your selection of poetry. Write the titles in the left-hand column, then different themes and techniques along the top. Work through each poem, ticking which themes and techniques appear. To develop your skills, make the boxes on your table big enough to add key quotations as evidence.

1. How many poems will you be comparing in the exam?
2. What two things might influence your choice of poem?
3. What should you do in the last paragraph of your answer?

First Impressions: Themes

➤ In your exam you will be expected to analyse a poem you have never seen before, and then compare it with another unseen poem.

➤ When you're given an unseen poem to analyse, start by reading it through and deciding, simply, what the poem is about.

➤ Think also about the speaker's viewpoint (this could be the poet's voice, or they could be taking on the narrative voice of a character).

➤ Once you've decided on the poem's themes and ideas, you're in a position to explain how the poet gets this across to the reader through language, **form** and structure.

TIFS

➤ A good way to analyse a poem, and help you structure your response, is to think about TIFS: themes, imagery, form, structure.

Horned Poppy

by *Vicki Feaver*

Frailest of flowers, armoured to survive
at the edge of the sea: leaves
tough as holly, hugging the stem
like spiked cuffs; the buds protected
by a prickly sheath; the petals furled
like yellow parachute silk, opening to expose,
at its radiant heart, the threads
of stamens, pollen's loose dust.
It blooms for at the most an hour;
torn apart by the elements it loves.
And then the pistil grows:
a live bootlace, a fuse
of multiplying cells – reaching out
to feel between the shingle's
sharp-edged flints for a moist bed
to lay its seed; or in my kitchen,
drying in the heat, a long thin hand
summoning a salt gale, a tide to roll in
over the flat land, roaring
through the open door.

*stamen / pistil = the reproductive organs of a flower
*shingle = the small pebbles on a beach

In response to the poem opposite, a student might write:

<u>Themes</u>
➤ Nature. The poet seems impressed by the flower but also sorry for it. She may be a bit guilty for taking it home (away from its natural environment).

<u>Imagery</u>
➤ Contrasting adjectives (frailest/armoured) – feels sorry for it, but is also impressed.
➤ Alliteration (frailest of flowers) – highlights the flower's vulnerability.
➤ Contrasting verbs (blooms / torn apart) – it's beautiful but quickly destroyed.
➤ Similes (tough as holly / like spike cuffs) to explore the impressive, strong side.
➤ Simile (like silk) to explore the gentle side.
➤ Metaphor (radiant heart) – she thinks it's beautiful/ impressive.
➤ Metaphor (live bootlace) – helps us imagine the pistil growing; she's fascinated by its life-cycle.
➤ Personification (long thin hand) – makes it seem old/weak/ desperate to suggest maybe she shouldn't have taken it home.

<u>Form</u>
➤ The **meter** isn't uniform which makes the poem look a bit ragged. This lack of uniformity can also be seen in the blank verse and enjambment. This could represent the wild, unprotected environment that the poppy grows in (which impresses the poet but also makes her sorry for the poppy, as it's eventually 'torn apart by the elements').

<u>Structure</u>
➤ Quite short, two-line sentence in the middle of the poem – emphasises the poet's main feelings of admiration and sadness.
➤ Lists of descriptions – builds up a detailed picture of the flower.
➤ Lots of short **clauses** in the first half of the poem – creates a series of dramatic pauses that suggest something (bad) is going to happen.

Form ➤
the type of a poem, such as a sonnet or a ballad. This includes the shape of a poem: the number of stanzas, the number of lines in those stanzas (for example, two lines = a couplet; four lines = a quatrain), whether there is a rhyme scheme, whether there is a clear meter, etc.

Meter ➤
the number of syllables/beats per line.

Clauses ➤
the parts of a sentence, each separated by punctuation.

19

Choose any poem (from the internet, or a section of the poetry anthology that you haven't studied). Stick it onto the middle of a sheet of A3 paper. Using different colours for the four areas of TIFS, annotate the things you notice about the poem.

1. What does TIFS stand for?
2. Every time you identify a feature of language or structure, what do you need to link it to?
3. What is form?

Sticking With TIFS

➤ The poems you are given to analyse in your exam could have been written at any time in the past. Older poems may seem more difficult at first sight because of the language used, but you will not be given anything too obscure. As with more modern poems, explore themes, imagery, form and structure.

➤ You could get a question like this: How does Wordsworth present the city of London in his poem?

Composed upon Westminster Bridge, September 3, 1802

by *William Wordsworth*

Earth has not anything to show more fair:
Dull would he be of soul who could pass by
A sight so touching in its majesty:
This City now doth, like a garment, wear
The beauty of the morning; silent, bare,
Ships, towers, domes, theatres, and temples lie
Open unto the fields, and to the sky;
All bright and glittering in the smokeless air.
Never did sun more beautifully steep
In his first splendour, valley, rock, or hill;
Ne'er saw I, never felt, a calm so deep!
The river glideth at his own sweet will:
Dear God! the very houses seem asleep;
And all that mighty heart is lying still!

Themes

➤ What city is Wordsworth writing about?

➤ What does he feel about this place?

Imagery

➤ Look for a simile. Look for any personification. How do these help to describe London?

➤ Look for any positive adjectives and adverbs. Why has Wordsworth used them?

➤ What feeling does Wordsworth describe towards the end of the poem, and why might this be surprising?

Form

➤ The poem has 14 lines, 10 syllables per line, and a clear rhyme scheme. Do you recognise this form? Why is this particularly suitable for Wordsworth's theme?

Structure

➤ Find a list. How is it being used?

➤ What word does he repeat and why?

➤ Where does Wordsworth use an exclamation and what does this convey?

Writing Your Analysis

➤ Start with a simple introduction that states the themes you've identified, for example:
Wordsworth is describing how beautiful and impressive the city of London is at sunrise.

➤ Explain how these themes are conveyed through imagery, for example:
One way in which Wordsworth conveys the beauty of London is through a combination of personification and simile, 'This City now doth like a garment wear / The beauty of the morning'. The image of clothes and the **abstract noun** *'beauty' suggest that London looks perfectly presented. Describing the city as a person is quite striking, which helps to show the impact that the city has had on the writer.*
Wordsworth also uses positive adjectives and adverbs to emphasise his love of London, 'fair... bright and glittering... beautifully'. These words all link to beauty, as if he sees the city as an attractive woman. The use of 'bright and glittering' links to richness (perhaps like a woman's jewellery), which suggests that Wordsworth values the city highly.

➤ Comment on the relevance of the form used by the poet, for example:
Wordsworth's choice of a sonnet is significant. He wants to convey his love of London, so he has chosen a form of love poetry. With its 14 lines, 10 syllables per line, and rhyme scheme, this is also a tightly constructed form, which could reflect how London is a packed, man-made city rather than a piece of nature.

➤ Explore how the poet has used structure, for example:
Wordsworth uses a list form to describe London, 'Ships, towers, domes, theatres, and temples'. This builds up our impression of the city so we can share Wordsworth's feelings. He includes very different shapes and places so we can visualise how diverse it is.
He continues to show how impressed he is by the use of an exclamation, 'Dear God!'. Coupled with the biblical language, this suggests that he is almost shocked by how wonderful the city is, but also, through the link to prayer, that he sees it as a gift from God.

20

> **Abstract noun ➤**
> an idea or feeling (like love, happiness, or time); unlike a regular noun, it cannot be held or touched.

Practise your poetry techniques. Make two cardboard dice and write different techniques of language and structure on their faces. Throw the dice and try to write a description of something in your room using the two techniques that come up.

1. What four things should you focus on when analysing an unseen poem?
2. What three things should you try to do in each paragraph of your analysis?
3. What is a sonnet?

Getting Started

➤ In your exam you will be given a second poem to compare to the one you have already analysed. Every point you make in your answer should mention a similarity or difference between the two poems.

➤ Read the second poem and think about TIFS: theme, imagery, form and structure.

➤ You then need to find some points of comparison.

Ideas for Comparison

➤ The exam question may state a theme, such as nature or friendship, but you still need to find three or four ideas within that. For example, one idea might be that the poets are fascinated by nature, and another that nature can be frightening, etc. Alternatively, you might have two poets who have different ideas about friendship: one may explore friendship formed as a child, while the other explores an adult friendship; one may conclude that friends are the most important thing, whilst the other may believe family comes first.

➤ Each of your ideas will allow you to build up a paragraph of comparison.

Quotation from poem 1 showing this idea

Analysis of how your quotation uses language or structure to convey this idea

Comparison idea about the two poems (a similarity or difference)

A connective of comparison, linking poem 1 to poem 2

Analysis of how your quotation uses language or structure to convey this idea

Quotation from poem 2 showing your idea

Imperative ➤ an order.

Colloquialism ➤ an everyday or slang phrase.

Superlative adjective ➤ an adjective that describes the most something can be (e.g. smallest).

Exploring Two Poems

➤ Look at these two short poems. They are both about sea life, but what other comparison ideas could you come up with? How could you analyse the ways in which language and structure are used to show these ideas?

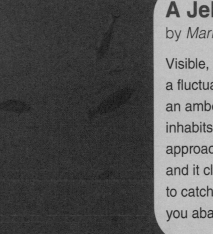

Fish
by Mary Ann Hoberman

Look at them flit
Lickety-split
Wiggling
Swiggling
Swerving
Curving
Hurrying
Scurrying
Chasing
Racing
Whizzing
Whisking
Flying
Frisking
Tearing around
With a leap and a bound
But none of them making the tiniest
       tiniest
       tiniest
       tiniest
       tiniest
       Sound

A Jelly-Fish
by Marianne Moore

Visible, invisible,
a fluctuating charm
an amber-tinctured amethyst
inhabits it, your arm
approaches and it opens
and it closes; you had meant
to catch it and it quivers;
you abandon your intent.

➤ Both are fascinated by the creatures. Moore shows this through contrast and metaphor, whilst Hoberman uses an **imperative** and a **colloquialism** about their speed.
➤ Both describe how the sea life moves. Moore uses a verb and metaphor, whilst Hoberman uses a list of rhyming verbs.
➤ The jellyfish is ultimately a bit scary, whilst the fish seem small and vulnerable. Moore uses a verb and a short clause for emphasis, whilst Hoberman uses repetition of a **superlative adjective**.
➤ Both use form to reflect their subject. Moore's poem is only eight lines long with similar length lines, making it look small and compact like the jellyfish. Hoberman's use of single word lines represents individual fish, whilst the indented lines at the end suggest the fish darting away from her or getting quieter.

Find two poems that are on a similar theme. Decide what the two poems are about. Cut them up and stick key lines for comparison next to each other. Make a set of similarities and a set of differences. Use a highlighter to identify techniques of language and structure.

1. What do you need to use to link your ideas?
2. What is a colloquialism?

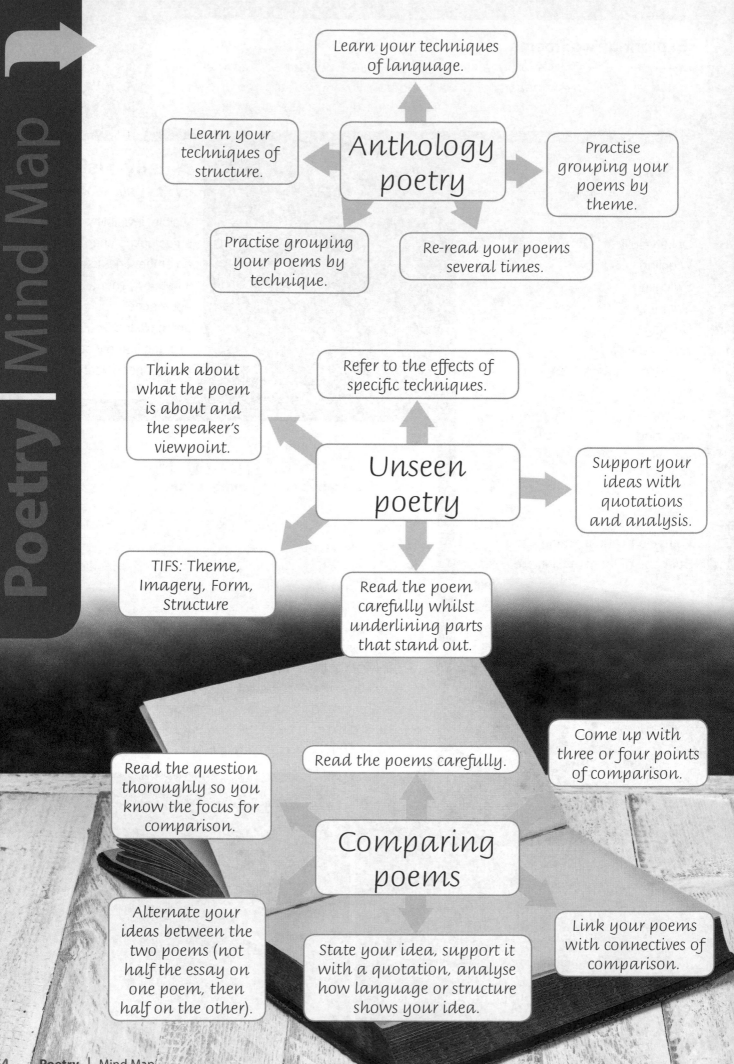

Learn your techniques of language.

Learn your techniques of structure.

Anthology poetry

Practise grouping your poems by theme.

Practise grouping your poems by technique.

Re-read your poems several times.

Think about what the poem is about and the speaker's viewpoint.

Refer to the effects of specific techniques.

Unseen poetry

Support your ideas with quotations and analysis.

TIFS: Theme, Imagery, Form, Structure

Read the poem carefully whilst underlining parts that stand out.

Read the question thoroughly so you know the focus for comparison.

Read the poems carefully.

Come up with three or four points of comparison.

Comparing poems

Alternate your ideas between the two poems (not half the essay on one poem, then half on the other).

State your idea, support it with a quotation, analyse how language or structure shows your idea.

Link your poems with connectives of comparison.

Anthology Poems

1. Love and Relationships

Compare the way poets present changing feelings in 'When We Two Parted' and one other poem from 'Love and Relationships'.

[30 marks]

2. Power and Conflict

Compare the way poets present suffering in 'London' and one other poem from 'Power and Conflict'.

[30 marks]

When We Two Parted
Lord Byron

When we two parted
In silence and tears
Half broken-hearted
To sever for years,
Pale grew thy cheek and cold,
Colder thy kiss;
Truly that hour foretold
Sorrow to this.

The dew of the morning
Sank chill on my brow-
It felt like the warning
Of what I feel now.
Thy vows are all broken.
And light is thy fame;
I hear thy name spoken,
And share in its shame.

They name thee before me,
A knell in mine ear,
A shudder come o'er me-
Why wert thou so dear?
They know not I know thee,
Who knew thee too well-
Long, long shall I rue thee,
Too deeply to tell.

In secret we met-
In silence I grieve,
That thy heart could forget,
Thy spirit deceive.
If I should meet thee
After long years,
How should I greet thee?-
With silence and tears

London
William Blake

I wander through each chartered street,
Near where the chartered Thames does flow,
And mark in every face I meet
Marks of weakness, marks of woe.

In every cry of every man,
In every infant's cry of fear,
In every voice, in every ban,
The mind-forged manacles I hear.

How the chimney-sweeper's cry
Every black'ning church appals
And the hapless soldier's sigh

Runs in blood down palace walls.

But most through midnight streets I hear
How the youthful harlot's curse
Blasts the new-born infant's tear,
And blights with plagues the marriage hearse.

Read 'Daughter' by Ellen Bryant Voigt.

Daughter *by Ellen Bryant Voigt*

There is one grief worse than any other.

When your small feverish throat clogged,
and quit
I knelt beside the chair on the green rug
and shook you and shook you,
but the only sound was mine shouting you back,
the delicate curls at your temples,
the blue wool blanket,
your face blue,
your jaw clamped against remedy—

how could I put a knife to that white neck?
With you in my lap,
my hands fluttering like flags,
I bend instead over your dead weight
to administer a kiss so urgent, so ruthless,
pumping breath into your stilled body,
counting out the rhythm for how long until
the second birth, the second cry
oh Jesus that sudden noisy musical inhalation
that leaves me stunned
by your survival.

1. In 'Daughter', the poet's child almost chokes to death. How does the poet convey her feelings about her daugher?   **[24 marks]**

Read 'Her First Week' by Sharon Olds.

Her First Week *by Sharon Olds*

She was so small I would scan the crib a half-second
to find her, face-down in a corner, limp
as something gently flung down, or fallen
from some sky an inch above the mattress. I would
tuck her arm along her side
and slowly turn her over. She would tumble
over part by part, like a load
of damp laundry, in the dryer, I'd slip
a hand in, under her neck,
slide the other under her back,
and evenly lift her up. Her little bottom
sat in my palm, her chest contained
the puckered, moire sacs, and her neck -
I was afraid of her neck, once I almost
thought I heard it quietly snap,
I looked at her and she swivelled her slate
eyes and looked at me. It was in
my care, the creature of her spine, like the first
chordate, as if the history
of the vertebrate had been placed in my hands.

Every time I checked, she was still
with us - someday, there would be a human
race. I could not see it in her eyes,
but when I fed her, gathered her
like a loose bouquet to my side and offered
the breast, greyish-white, and struck with
minuscule scars like creeks in sunlight, I
felt she was serious, I believed she was willing to stay.

2. In both 'Daugher' and 'Her First Week', the poets express their feelings about
   their children. What are the similarities and differences between the ways the
   poets present their feelings? **[8 marks]**

First Impressions

Start by revising who your key characters are and their **characteristics** at the start of the play. For example:

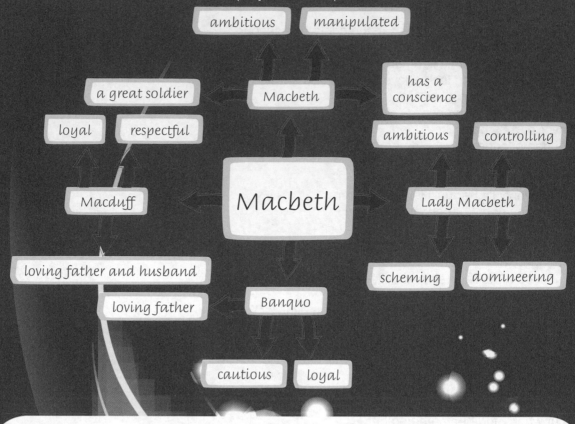

- ambitious
- manipulated
- a great soldier
- Macbeth
- has a conscience
- loyal
- respectful
- ambitious
- controlling
- Macduff
- **Macbeth**
- Lady Macbeth
- loving father and husband
- scheming
- domineering
- loving father
- Banquo
- cautious
- loyal

First Impressions: Evidence

➤ For all your ideas, you need to think about how Shakespeare shows this.

➤ You don't need to learn big chunks of the play, but try to remember key events and learn some key words. For example:

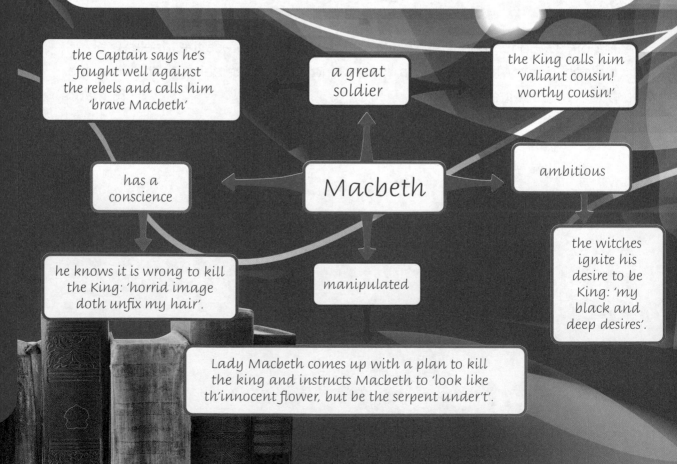

- the Captain says he's fought well against the rebels and calls him 'brave Macbeth'
- a great soldier
- the King calls him 'valiant cousin! worthy cousin!'
- has a conscience
- **Macbeth**
- ambitious
- he knows it is wrong to kill the King: 'horrid image doth unfix my hair'.
- manipulated
- the witches ignite his desire to be King: 'my black and deep desires'.
- Lady Macbeth comes up with a plan to kill the king and instructs Macbeth to 'look like th'innocent flower, but be the serpent under't'.

Development

➤ Once you have established what your character is like at the start of the play, you need to think about how your character is developed.

➤ Does Shakespeare give more examples of a specific characteristic?

➤ Does Shakespeare change the character in any way?

➤ Try to link your ideas to specific events in the play and key words or phrases from the text. For example:

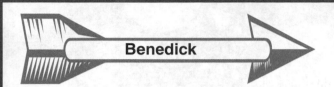

In *Much Ado About Nothing*, Benedick begins the play as comical, rude, unromantic and disliking Beatrice. Later he becomes romantic ('I have railed so long against marriage: but does not the appetite alter?'), in love with Beatrice ('I do with an eye of love requite her'; marrying her) and heroic (agreeing to a duel with Claudio for Beatrice).

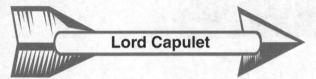

At the start of *Romeo and Juliet*, Lord Capulet is shown to be powerful and aggressive, but a loving father. However, later on he tries to calm the Capulet/Montague feud (ordering Tybalt to ignore Romeo at the party). He becomes cruel to Juliet ('Hang! Beg! Starve! Die in the streets!'), but he makes friends with the Montagues at the end ('Brother Montague, give me thy hand').

Characteristics ➤
what a person is like (their behaviour, thoughts, and attitudes).

Stick two pieces of A3 paper together to create a long sheet of paper. Sketch each of your characters down the left-hand side. Then create a timeline for each character, sketching key events, including key quotations, and noting how the characters change. Add a sketch on the far-right of your sheet, showing how the characters end the play (such as happily married or dead).

What two things should you consider about your main characters?

Pick who you think is the most important character in your play; what are they like at the start?

How do they develop and how does the play show you this?

Identifying Themes

➤ Start by deciding on four or five key themes that appear in the play you've studied. For example:

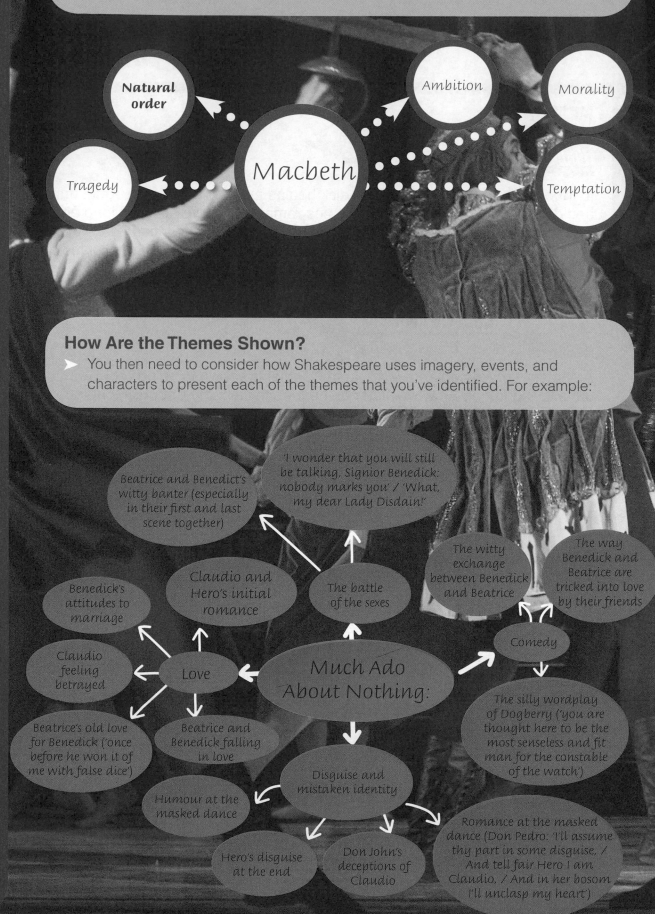

Natural order

Ambition

Morality

Macbeth

Tragedy

Temptation

How Are the Themes Shown?

➤ You then need to consider how Shakespeare uses imagery, events, and characters to present each of the themes that you've identified. For example:

Beatrice and Benedict's witty banter (especially in their first and last scene together)

'I wonder that you will still be talking, Signior Benedick: nobody marks you' / 'What, my dear Lady Disdain!'

The witty exchange between Benedick and Beatrice

The way Benedick and Beatrice are tricked into love by their friends

Benedick's attitudes to marriage

Claudio and Hero's initial romance

The battle of the sexes

Comedy

Claudio feeling betrayed

Love

Much Ado About Nothing:

The silly wordplay of Dogberry ('you are thought here to be the most senseless and fit man for the constable of the watch')

Beatrice's old love for Benedick ('once before he won it of me with false dice')

Beatrice and Benedick falling in love

Disguise and mistaken identity

Humour at the masked dance

Hero's disguise at the end

Don John's deceptions of Claudio

Romance at the masked dance (Don Pedro: 'I'll assume thy part in some disguise, / And tell fair Hero I am Claudio, / And in her bosom I'll unclasp my heart')

23

Practise Writing About the Themes

➤ If you get a question on how Shakespeare presents a theme, you need to be able to explain where it appears, how characters are used to explore it, and any references to language that you can remember. You don't need to use lots of quotations, but some key phrases will look very good.

➤ Read the first paragraph of a student response to a question about how Shakespeare presents the theme of conflict in *Romeo and Juliet*. Notice that it doesn't just describe the conflicts in the play. The student makes specific references to parts of the play, uses key words, and suggests what Shakespeare is saying about conflict.

> Shakespeare introduces the theme of conflict in the Prologue. He establishes the main conflict between the Montagues and Capulets, describing it as an 'ancient grudge'. This suggests they can't even remember why they are fighting. Shakespeare makes references to 'blood' and 'death' to highlight the effects of conflict. He develops this in the first scene of the play with the fight between the families based on a silly insult but quickly escalating as more people (such as Benvolio and Tybalt) get involved. We see how the conflict comes from the parents as well as the children, with Lord Capulet demanding to be brought his 'long sword' so he can join in the fight. However, Shakespeare shows that not everyone wants conflict, with both wives trying to calm their husbands.
>
> Shakespeare explores the theme of conflict further at the Capulet ball...

Natural order ➤
the idea that the King was chosen by God, and that his line of descendants shouldn't be interrupted.

Make a theme poster for your play. Use different symbols and sketches to represent each theme and how it's shown through character and events.
To develop your skills, add key quotations to help you think about Shakespeare's use of language.

What are the main themes in the play you've studied?

What do you think is the most important theme in the play and why?

When writing about a theme, what areas should you focus on?

Setting

➤ Setting is the time and place in which the play is set. For example:
  ➤ *Much Ado About Nothing*   16th century Messina (a port of Sicily)
  ➤ *Macbeth*   11th century Scotland
  ➤ *Romeo and Juliet*   14th/15th century Verona, Italy

Context

➤ Context refers to the historical events, attitudes, beliefs and behaviour that affect a piece of writing.
➤ When looking at a Shakespeare play, you should think about the context of Elizabethan/Jacobean England (when Shakespeare was writing), as well as the context of the play's setting. For example:

James I's
interest in the
supernatural

Traditional
expectations
of women

Macbeth

The **divine right**
of kingship

Limited medical
knowledge

24

You need to think about how the contexts present within the play you have studied are affecting what is happening on stage. For example:

Macbeth

The divine right of kingship:
- The references to bad weather
- Macbeth's fears about killing the king
- His feelings of guilt after killing the king and thinking he will never rest
- The witches and their supernatural powers
- The appearance of Banquo's ghost
- Lady Macbeth's madness
- The re-establishment of correct order at the end

➤ Look at this extract from Act 2 scene 2 of *Macbeth*, after he has killed the King. How do you think the play's context shows us things about Macbeth and Lady Macbeth?

MACBETH One cried 'God bless us!' and 'Amen' the other;

As they had seen me with these hangman's hands.

Listening their fear, I could not say 'Amen,'

When they did say 'God bless us!'

LADY MACBETH Consider it not so deeply.

MACBETH But wherefore could not I pronounce 'Amen'?

I had most need of blessing, and 'Amen'

Stuck in my throat.

LADY MACBETH These deeds must not be thought

After these ways; so, it will make us mad.

MACBETH Methought I heard a voice cry 'Sleep no more!

Macbeth does murder sleep', the innocent sleep,

Sleep that knits up the ravell'd sleeve of care,

The death of each day's life, sore labour's bath,

Balm of hurt minds, great nature's second course,

Chief nourisher in life's feast,--

Macbeth's shock that he 'could not say Amen', reminds us that the play is set at a time when people were more religious. The murder of the King is a sin and this is increased for Macbeth because he would have believed in the divine right of kings, so his murder of Duncan is also an attack on God. He knows he is in need of 'blessing' because he has damned himself to Hell. The idea that he has upset the natural order of the world can be seen in his metaphorical descriptions of sleep and its 'murder'. Because of what he has done, 'great nature' will be against him and he will not get the rest and peace of mind that comes with sleep.

Lady Macbeth's response to his fears emphasise her as unwomanly for the time the play was written and set. Rather than taking his views on board and appearing submissive, she takes control and dismisses his words in short **imperative** sentences.

the idea that the king was chosen by God, and that his line of descendants should not be interrupted.

a view of normality based on what has often been done in the past.

an order.

Using pictures from old magazines and the internet, make a collage that represents the setting and contexts of the play you have studied. To develop your skills, stick key quotations onto the pictures that give evidence of how the setting and context are affecting the play.

What is context?

What are the setting and contexts of the play you are studying?

What does traditional mean?

Getting Started

➤ When responding to an extract, you need to be more detailed and analytical because you have the text in front of you.

➤ Underline parts of the text that relate to the exam question and highlight specific techniques like metaphors, etc.

Analysing Character and Language

➤ Think about what the character is like and, considering where the extract is from in the play, whether the character has changed in any way. Then explore where you can find evidence for these characteristics in the extract.

➤ Look at these two short extracts of speech and the annotations done by a student.

MACBETH (ACT 3 SCENE 4)

MACBETH Then comes my fit again:
I had else been perfect;

Whole as the marble, founded as the rock,

As broad and general as the casing air:

But now, I am cabin'd, cribb'd, confin'd, bound in

To saucy doubts and fears. – But Banquo's safe?

Since killing Duncan, Macbeth has been restless/nervous.

Pattern of three – he wants to feel secure.

Metaphor for paranoia.

Alliteration of harsh c sound – sound violent to emphasise his paranoia.

Irony in use of 'safe' (he's checking Banquo's dead) – he's lost his previous values of brotherhood, etc.

ROMEO AND JULIET (ACT 3 SCENE 1)

LADY CAPULET Tybalt, my cousin,
O my brother's child!

O Prince, O husband, O, the blood is spill'd

Of my dear kinsman. Prince, as thou art true,

For blood of ours shed blood of Montague.

O cousin, cousin.

Repetition of 'blood' – the death has made her more aggressive.

Adjective 'dear' – she loved Tybalt as a family member.

Imperative demanding Romeo's death – she's stronger/more confident than earlier.

Repetition of 'cousin' and the exclamatory 'O' – Lady Capulet grieves over Tybalt's death. (see top line also)

Writing About Character and Language

➤ Write clear, concise, analytical paragraphs. A good structure to follow is:

1. State your point about the character (you might also link this to where the extract comes from in the play).

2. Provide a brief quotation from the extract as evidence.

3. Analyse how the language and/or structure in your quotation shows the point that you made about character.

4. Using a connective phrase, either develop your point with another quotation and analysis or start a new point and repeat the process.

➤ A paragraph of analysis using the structure above might look like this:

MUCH ADO ABOUT NOTHING (ACT 1 SCENE 3)

DON JOHN I had rather be a canker in a hedge than a rose in his grace, and it better fits my blood to be disdained of all that to fashion a carriage to rob love from any.

*Don John prefers to be an outsider, 'rather be a canker in a hedge than a rose'. By having him compare himself to a wild rose, Shakespeare reminds us of his illegitimacy and the **stigma** of this at the time. Similarly, Don John explains his wish to remain an outsider when he says, 'better fits my blood to be disdained of all that to fashion a carriage to rob love'. The metaphorical language shows that he refuses to change himself in order to be liked. The word 'blood' links again to his illegitimacy, suggesting he is very aware of how people view him.*

Pattern of three ➤
grouping three ideas together for emphasis.

Irony ➤
saying one thing but actually having the opposite meaning.

Stigma ➤
something that people see as a mark of disgrace.

Working with a friend, pick out three quotations for each other that show what a character is like. Write each one in the centre of a piece of A4 paper. Swap, annotate, and analyse them. Afterwards, discuss your ideas with each other.

How is your response to an extract expected to be different to your response to the whole text?

What do you need to do every time you've backed an idea up with a quotation?

What is irony?

Getting Started

➤ As with responding to an extract on character, you need to be detailed and analytical.

➤ Read the question carefully, then read the extract a few times and make annotations.

Analysing Theme and Language

➤ Think about how characters and events are presenting the theme, and how Shakespeare achieves this through language and structure.

➤ Look at this extract and a student's annotations, exploring how Shakespeare presents the theme of manipulation.

MACBETH (ACT 1 SCENE 7)

MACBETH We will proceed no further in this business:

He hath honour'd me of late; and I have bought

Golden opinions from all sorts of people,

Which would be worn now in their newest gloss,

Not cast aside so soon.

LADY MACBETH Was the hope drunk

Wherein you dress'd yourself? hath it slept since?

And wakes it now, to look so green and pale

At what it did so freely? From this time

Such I account thy love. Art thou afeard

To be the same in thine own act and valour

As thou art in desire? Wouldst thou have that

Which thou esteem'st the ornament of life,

And live a coward in thine own esteem,

Letting 'I dare not' wait upon 'I would,'

Like the poor cat i' the adage?

MACBETH Prithee, peace.

I dare do all that may become a man;

Who dares do more is none.

LADY MACBETH What beast was't, then,

That made you break this enterprise to me?

Confident statement – Macbeth is trying to take control.

Verb 'honour'd' and metaphor 'golden opinions' – Macbeth gives his reasons why he won't kill Duncan.

Pattern of three **rhetorical questions** – she mocks his change of heart and calls him cowardly.

Short sentence – claims he doesn't love her (emotional blackmail).

More rhetorical questions to make him change his mind again.

Words linked to weakness to shame him – 'afeard', 'coward', 'I dare not'.

Compares him to a small, unmanly animal.

Short sentence – Macbeth tries to take control.

Repetition of verb 'dare' – he's trying to argue back.

Use of irony to shame him – he's not a powerful beast (he's the small cat from her previous line).

When you durst do it, then you were a man;

And, to be more than what you were, you would

Be so much more the man. Nor time nor place

Did then adhere, and yet you would make both:

They have made themselves, and that their fitness now

Does unmake you. I have given suck, and know

How tender 'tis to love the babe that milks me:

I would, while it was smiling in my face,

Have pluck'd my nipple from his boneless gums,

And dash'd the brains out, had I so sworn as you

Have done to this.

MACBETH If we should fail?

Repetition of 'man' – again to make him feel unmanly. **Past tense** *to show he's being weak;* **conditional tense** *to suggest he can change.*

Verb 'unmake' – he's unmanly.

Vivid, horrific image, emphasised by verb 'dash'd' – suggesting she's stronger than Macbeth. Implies he's more like the 'babe'.

Verb 'sworn' – pointing out he's broken a promise.

The question shows Macbeth is still worried, but is again thinking about killing the king.

Write clear, concise, analytical paragraphs: state an idea, support it with a quotation from the text, analyse how the language or structure in your quotation shows your idea. For example:

The first way Lady Macbeth manipulates Macbeth is by suggesting he is a coward, 'Was the hope drunk / Wherein you dress'd yourself? hath it slept since? / And wakes it now, to look so green and pale / At what it did so freely?' She uses a pattern of three rhetorical questions to make Macbeth feel accused, including references to colours that symbolise cowardice (emphasised by the mocking adverb 'so') and the verb 'slept' to suggest he's passive not active.

She continues to imply his cowardice by using words that link to weakness…

Rhetorical question ➤

a question asked to make an audience think rather than answer.

Conditional tense ➤

describing things that would happen, dependent on some condition.

Past tense ➤

describing things that have happened.

Print off an extract from your play. Cut up the lines to space them out, and stick them to a piece of paper. Highlight techniques of language and structure, then add annotations about theme underneath each line.

Choose a theme from your play. What scenes does this theme appear in?

When exploring how character and events show a theme, what do you need to analyse?

What is a rhetorical question?

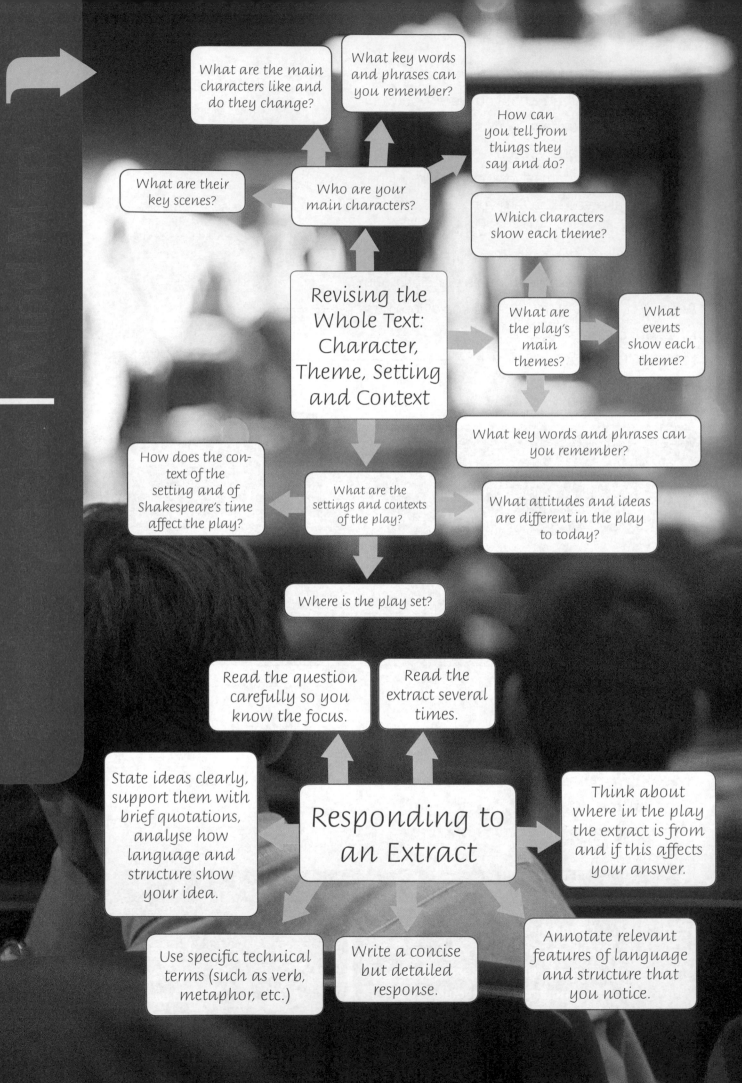

What are the main characters like and do they change?

What key words and phrases can you remember?

How can you tell from things they say and do?

What are their key scenes?

Who are your main characters?

Which characters show each theme?

Revising the Whole Text: Character, Theme, Setting and Context

What are the play's main themes?

What events show each theme?

What key words and phrases can you remember?

How does the context of the setting and of Shakespeare's time affect the play?

What are the settings and contexts of the play?

What attitudes and ideas are different in the play to today?

Where is the play set?

Read the question carefully so you know the focus.

Read the extract several times.

State ideas clearly, support them with brief quotations, analyse how language and structure show your idea.

Responding to an Extract

Think about where in the play the extract is from and if this affects your answer.

Use specific technical terms (such as verb, metaphor, etc.)

Write a concise but detailed response.

Annotate relevant features of language and structure that you notice.

MUCH ADO ABOUT NOTHING (ACT 2 SCENE 3)

Read the following extract from *Much Ado About Nothing*.

BENEDICK I do much wonder that one man, seeing how much another man is a fool when he dedicates his behaviours to love, will, after he hath laughed at such shallow follies in others, become the argument of his own scorn by failing in love: and such a man is Claudio. I have known when there was no music with him but the drum and the fife; and now had he rather hear the tabor and the pipe: I have known when he would have walked ten mile a-foot to see a good armour; and now will he lie ten nights awake, carving the fashion of a new doublet. He was wont to speak plain and to the purpose, like an honest man and a soldier; and now is he turned orthography; his words are a very fantastical banquet, just so many strange dishes. May I be so converted and see with these eyes? I cannot tell; I think not: I will not be sworn, but love may transform me to an oyster; but I'll take my oath on it, till he have made an oyster of me, he shall never make me such a fool. One woman is fair, yet I am well; another is wise, yet I am well; another virtuous, yet I am well; but till all graces be in one woman, one woman shall not come in my grace. Rich she shall be, that's certain; wise, or I'll none; virtuous, or I'll never cheapen her; fair, or I'll never look on her; mild, or come not near me; noble, or not I for an angel; of good discourse, an excellent musician, and her hair shall be of what colour it please God. Ha! the prince and Monsieur Love! I will hide me in the arbour.

1. Starting with this extract, how far do you think that Shakespeare presents Benedick as a dislikeable character?

   Write about:

   • How Shakespeare presents Benedick in this speech

   • How Shakespeare presents Benedick in the play as a whole.

   [30] + (A04) [4]

MACBETH (ACT 1 SCENE 3)

Read the following extract from *Macbeth* and then answer the questions that follow. Here, Ross and Angus bring the news that Macbeth has been made Thane of Cawdor.

> **ROSS** The king hath happily received, Macbeth,
> The news of thy success; and when he reads
> Thy personal venture in the rebels' fight,
> His wonders and his praises do contend
> Which should be thine or his: silenced with that,
> In viewing o'er the rest o' the selfsame day,
> He finds thee in the stout Norweyan ranks,
> Nothing afeard of what thyself didst make,
> Strange images of death. As thick as hail
> Came post with post; and every one did bear
> praises in his kingdom's great defence,
> And pour'd them down before him.
>
> **ANGUS** We are sent
> To give thee from our royal master thanks;
> Only to herald thee into his sight,
> Not pay thee.
>
> **ROSS** And, for an earnest of a greater honour,
> He bade me, from him, call thee thane of Cawdor:
> In which addition, hail, most worthy thane!
> For it is thine.
>
> **BANQUO** What, can the devil speak true?
>
> **MACBETH** The thane of Cawdor lives: why do you dress me
> In borrow'd robes?
>
> **ANGUS** Who was the thane lives yet;
> But under heavy judgment bears that life
> Which he deserves to lose. Whether he was combined
> With those of Norway, or did line the rebel
> With hidden help and vantage, or that with both
> He labour'd in his country's wreck,
> I know not;
> But treasons capital, confess'd and proved,
> Have overthrown him.
>
> **MACBETH** (*aside*) Glamis, and thane of Cawdor!
> The greatest is behind.

1. Starting with this extract, how far do you think Shakespeare presents Macbeth as a good man?

   Write about:

   • How Shakespeare presents Macbeth in this speech

   • How Shakespeare presents Macbeth in the play as a whole.

   [30] + (A04) [4]

ROMEO AND JULIET (ACT 1 SCENE 2)

Read the following extract from *Romeo and Juliet,* and then asnwer the questions that follow. Capulet and Paris are discussing Juliet's possible marriage to Paris.

CAPULET But saying o'er what I have said before:
My child is yet a stranger in the world;
She hath not seen the change of fourteen years,
Let two more summers wither in their pride,
Ere we may think her ripe to be a bride.
PARIS Younger than she are happy mothers made.
CAPULET And too soon marr'd are those so early made.
The earth hath swallow'd all my hopes but she,
She is the hopeful lady of my earth:
But woo her, gentle Paris, get her heart,
My will to her consent is but a part;
An she agree, within her scope of choice
Lies my consent and fair according voice.
This night I hold an old accustom'd feast,
Whereto I have invited many a guest,
Such as I love; and you, among the store,
One more, most welcome, makes my number more.
At my poor house look to behold this night
Earth-treading stars that make dark heaven light:
Such comfort as do lusty young men feel
When well-apparell'd April on the heel
Of limping winter treads, even such delight
Among fresh female buds shall you this night
Inherit at my house; hear all, all see,
And like her most whose merit most shall be:
Which on more view, of many mine being one
May stand in number, though in reckoning none,
Come, go with me.

1. Starting with this extract, how far do you think Shakespeare presents Lord Capulet as a caring father?

    Write about:

    • How Shakespeare presents Lord Capulet in this extract

    • How Shakespeare presents Lord Capulet in the play as a whole.

    [30] + (A04) [4]

What Main Characters are Like

➤ Start by thinking about who the main characters are, what they're like at the start of the book, and how you can tell what they're like. For example:

Unhappy childhood – orphaned; bullied by the Reeds; mistreated at Lowood by Mr Brocklehurst; about John Reed: 'every nerve I had feared him, and every morsel of flesh on my bones shrank when he came near'.

Determined – stands up to Mrs Reed; tries to better herself at Lowood; wants to be free and independent; 'a fondness for some of my studies, and a desire to excel in all'.

Jane Eyre

Caring – stays with Helen on her deathbed; cares for Adele; helps Rochester when he falls from his horse; 'I'll stay with you, dear Helen: no one shall take me away'.

Jane Eyre

Rude – he is initially rude to Jane; he is off-hand with Mrs Fairfax; he won't pretend to be nice in polite company; 'he would sometimes pass me haughtily or coldly'.

Edward Rochester

Passionate – he follows his heart rather than social conventions; 'I have a right to get pleasure out of life: and I will get it, cost what it may'.

Mysterious – we don't realise who he is at first; strange events in the house, such as the fire in his room; his strange relationship with Richard Mason; 'Mrs Fairfax either could not, or would not, give me more explicit information of the origin and nature of Mr Rochester's trials'.

➤ You need to revise which events in the novel are important for showing what your characters are like. It's a bonus if you can also learn some key quotations allowing you to analyse the writer's use of language.

Context ➤
the historical events, attitudes, beliefs and behaviour that affect a piece of writing (due to when it was written and/or set).

Characters and Context
➤ It's important to think about how the characters are affected by the context of the novel. This can help us to understand their behaviour or how others react to them. For example:

The Strange Case of Dr Jekyll and Mr Hyde – Dr Henry Jekyll

Victorian Values	How These Affect His Characterisation
Christianity	Jekyll sees Hyde as the battle between good and evil within him: 'the spirit of hell awoke in me and raged'. Hyde commits immoral crimes that shock Jekyll.
Proper social conduct	Jekyll, as a respected gentleman, cannot behave how he wants to; his experiments lead him to create Mr Hyde (allowing him to hide his improper conduct and 'pleasures').
Intolerance of crime	Shocked at the murder of Carew, Jekyll tries to resist becoming Hyde: 'I embraced anew the restrictions of natural life'.

How Main Characters Change

➤ Once you've established what your main characters are like, you need to explore how they change or develop. Think about how you can tell this from how the characters speak and behave during key scenes in the book. For example:

Great Expectations

- Unhappy childhood but loves Joe.
- Desperate for Estella to love him.

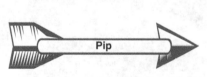

- Becomes a gentleman.
- Is ashamed of Joe.
- Increasingly selfish.
- Develops a conscience, is remorseful and works hard to make up for his mistakes.

Make your own character magazine. For each character, include: a sketch; fact-file; a timeline of what the character is like, how they change, and why; key quotes of description and speech. To develop your skills, choose a characteristic of each character and include a paragraph analysing how it's shown.

Who are the main characters in your novel?

2. What are these characters like and how do they change or develop?

3. How are they affected by the novel's context?

Identify Settings

➤ Start by identifying the main settings in your novel. Try to also identify some key quotations about each setting. For example:

'the dismal wilderness'

'this bleak place overgrown with nettles was the churchyard'

'on every rail and gate, wet lay clammy; and the marsh-mist was so thick'

'Mrs Joe was a very clean housekeeper, but had an exquisite art of making her cleanliness more uncomfortable and unacceptable than dirt itself'

The Kent marshes (including the churchyard)

'the dismal atmosphere of the place' [Mr Jaggers's room]

Great Expectations (set: mid-1800s)

Pip's home and the forge

Central London (including the law practice and Pip's lodgings)

'so crowded with people and so brilliantly lighted in the dusk of evening' [London streets]

'the place and the meal would have a more homely look than ever, and I would feel more ashamed of home than ever'

Satis House

'all asmear with filth and fat and blood and foam' [Smithfield]

'the daylight was completely excluded, and it had an airless smell that was oppressive'

'I felt as if the stopping of the clocks had stopped Time in that mysterious place, and, while I and everything outside it grew older, it stood still'

'heavily overhung with cobwebs'

How Settings are Presented

➤ Practise analysing how the author uses different features of language and structure to convey what different settings are like (their appearance and **atmosphere**). For example:

Charlotte Bronte presents Thornfield as unwelcoming, 'A very chill and vault-like air pervaded the stairs and gallery, suggesting cheerless ideas of space and solitude'.
Images of coldness are emphasised by the simile that links the house to a tomb, and by the verb 'pervaded' which suggests this unpleasant atmosphere is everywhere. This coldness is **literal** but also links to emotional coldness through the adjective 'cheerless' which makes it clear that the 'solitude' is lonely rather than peaceful.

Clear point about setting

Evidence containing interesting language

Analysis of how specific words and phrases link to the point being made about the setting

Atmosphere ➤
the emotion or feeling of a piece of writing.
Literal ➤
the basic, surface meaning.

What Settings Add to the Novel

➤ As well as being aware of how the settings are presented by the author, you should also revise how the settings help you understand things about the characters, themes, and context of the novel. For example:

The contrasts between the descriptions of the Kent marshes and central London in *Great Expectations* help us to explore the theme of class in the mid 1800s.

The descriptions of Thornfield in *Jane Eyre* show us aspects of Rochester's character.

In *The Strange Case of Dr Jekyll and Mr Hyde*, comparing the front and side entrance of Dr Jekyll's house links to the respectable, socially-acceptable facade that he puts on in life.

Create posters for each of your settings, either by drawing them or using images from magazines and the internet. Accompany your images with key quotations from the novel about each setting. To develop your skills, add extra labels (using two different colours) about how the settings link to character or theme.

What are the main settings in your novel?

How do the settings help to tell you about character?

How do the settings link to theme?

Identify Main Themes

➤ Start by identifying the main ideas that the writer is exploring in their novel. For example, in *Great Expectations*:

Family

Class and **Ambition**

Guilt

Love

Crime

Growing up

How Themes are Presented

➤ Decide which characters and events in your novel help to introduce or develop each of your themes. Find key quotations from the novel that show how the theme is expressed and consider whether the theme is being affected by the novel's context. For example:

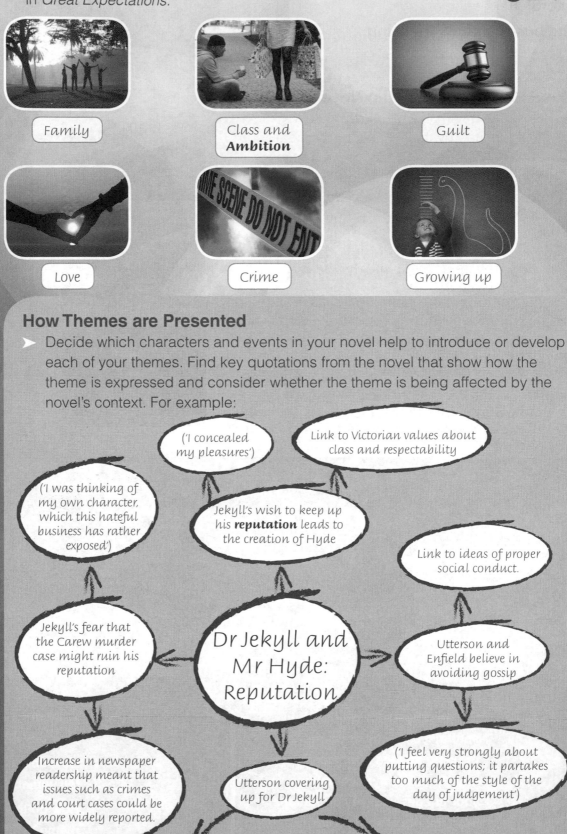

('I concealed my pleasures')

Link to Victorian values about class and respectability

('I was thinking of my own character, which this hateful business has rather exposed')

Jekyll's wish to keep up his **reputation** leads to the creation of Hyde

Link to ideas of proper social conduct.

Jekyll's fear that the Carew murder case might ruin his reputation

Dr Jekyll and Mr Hyde: Reputation

Utterson and Enfield believe in avoiding gossip

Increase in newspaper readership meant that issues such as crimes and court cases could be more widely reported.

Utterson covering up for Dr Jekyll

('I feel very strongly about putting questions; it partakes too much of the style of the day of judgement')

('I would say nothing of this paper. If your master has fled or is dead, we may at least save his credit')

Link to the importance of respectability and status.

How to Write About Themes

➤ Writing about themes is the same as writing about character or setting. Make clear points, support them with quotations as evidence, and analyse how the author's use of language or structure gets across the point you have made.

One way in which the theme of social class is presented in 'Jane Eyre' is through the way Jane thinks that she is not good enough for Rochester, 'I know I must conceal my sentiments: I must smother hope; I must remember that he cannot care much for me'. The use of the metaphor about smothering hope reminds us that love between the social classes was rare in Victorian England. This is emphasised by the verbs 'know' and 'remember' that imply people had a clear social position that they were aware of and should not try to move beyond. The use of the negative verb 'cannot' indicates that **social expectations** trap all classes as, here, they affect Rochester not Jane. The pattern of three, using the imperative verb 'must', suggests that Jane also fears for her job should the truth come out, which links to the vulnerability of women and the lower classes.

- Clear point about the theme
- Evidence
- Analysis of specific features of language or structure
- Links to context
- Further analysis if possible; not just moving on to the next point

Ambition ➤
desire to succeed in some way.

Reputation ➤
the opinions that people have formed about someone.

Social expectations ➤
how society expects people to behave.

On a sheet of A3 paper, create theme pyramids. You are only allowed one word for the top layer: this should be your theme, such as 'Love'. For the second layer, you are allowed two single words or a two-word phrase; for the third layer, you are allowed three words, etc. Using ten layers for each of your pyramids, try to summarise the main points about each theme in your novel.

1. What are the main themes in your novel?
2. How do they link to characters and events?
3. How do the novel's themes link to its context?

State an idea, support it with evidence, analyse how features of language or structure have conveyed your idea.

Who are your main characters and how do they develop?

What are the main settings of the novel? What can they tell you about characters?

The 19th Century Novel

What are the main themes of your novel? How are they shown through character, setting and events?

What key quotations can you find about character, setting and theme?

What are the contexts within your novel? How do they affect character and events?

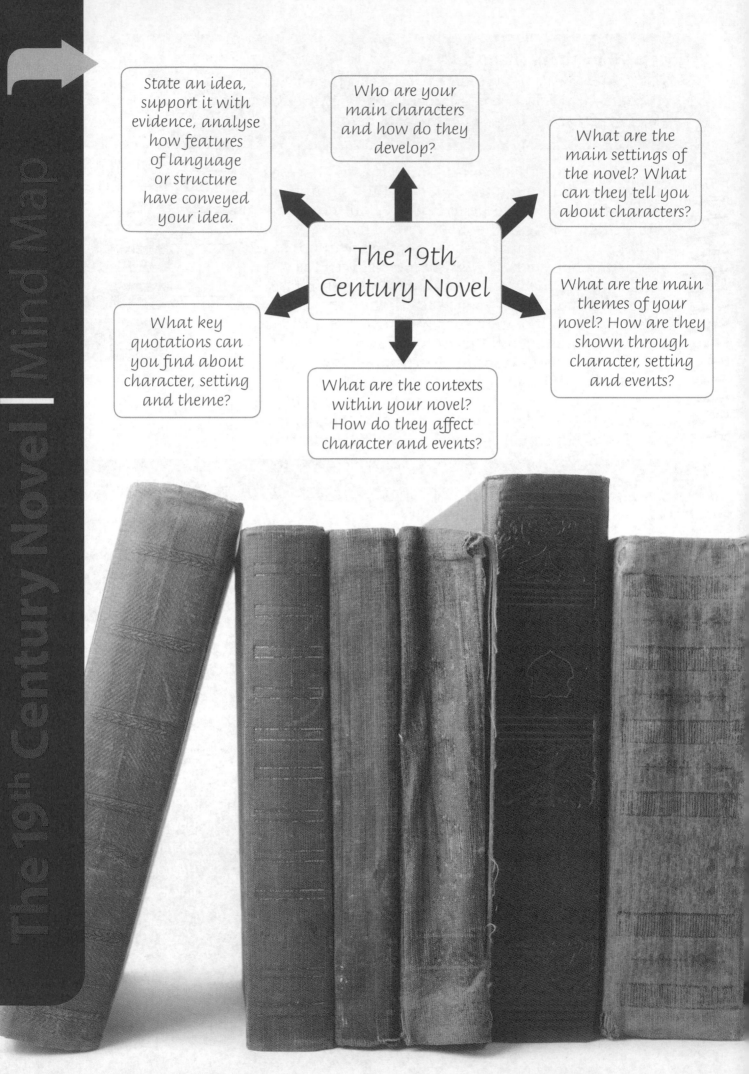

1. *The Strange Case of Dr Jekyll and Mr Hyde*

   Read the chapter entitled 'The Carew Murder Case' from the beginning to:
   At the horror of these sights and sounds, the maid fainted

   In the extract a maid witnesses Hyde committing murder.

   Starting with this extract, write about how Stevenson creates an atmosphere of horror through the characters of Dr Jekyll and Mr Hyde.

   Write about:
   *   how Stevenson creates an atmosphere of horror in this extract
   *   how he uses Dr Jekyll and Mr Hyde to create an atmosphere of horror in the novel as a whole. **[30 marks]**

2. *Great Expectations*

   Read Chapter 8 from:
   It was not in the first moments that I saw all these things, though I saw more of them in the first moments than might be supposed.
   To:
   Afterwards she kept her hands there for a little while, and slowly took them away as if they were heavy.

   In this extract Pip meets Miss Havisham for the first time.

   Starting with this extract, explain how Dickens presents Miss Havisham as a disturbing character.

   Write about:
   *   how Dickens describes Miss Havisham in the extract
   *   how he writes about Miss Havisham in the novel as a whole. **[30 marks]**

3. *Jane Eyre*

   Read Chapter 7 from:
   'Fetch that stool,' said Mr Brocklehurst
   To:
   'How shocking!'

   In this extract Jane is punished by Mr Brocklehurst.

   Starting with this extract, explain how Brontë presents the theme of cruelty in Jane Eyre.

   Write about:
   *   how Brontë presents cruelty in the extract
   *   how she presents cruelty in the novel as a whole. **[30 marks]**

   > To generate your own question, choose a character or theme in the novel you have studied. Find a short extract from the novel which features this character or theme and use it as a starting point. Then write about how your chosen character/theme is presented in the extract and in the novel as a whole.

The Main Characters
➤ Start by identifying your main characters and their characteristics at the start of the story. Think about:

Physical ➤ to do with the body.
Connectives ➤ joining words or phrases.
Consequence ➤ the effect or result of something.

their relationships

what others say about them

what they say and how they say it

Character

how the writer uses language to portray them

their actions

➤ Make sure you can evidence your ideas about character, either through key quotations or referring to specific events in the text. For example:

Lots of **physical** descriptions: 'the fat boy', 'he wiped his glasses and adjusted them on his button nose'; 'Piggy flushed suddenly'.

Jack is rude to Piggy as he sees him as inferior; Ralph begins to stand up for him ('Piggy's got the conch').

Piggy from *Lord of the Flies*

He's shy with people ('waited to be asked his name'); he likes Ralph, who grows to like him back; he's bullied by people like Jack ('Shut up, Fatty').

He tries to organise people (such as getting people's names at the start); he looks after the younger children ('Let him have the conch!') but gets annoyed when people are immature ('Like a crowd of kids').

He complains and sounds weak ('I can't swim. I wasn't allowed. My asthma –'); he's sensible and makes plans ('We can use this to call the others. Have a meeting.'); he's not as educated as the others ('All them other kids').

30

Character Development

➤ You should consider whether your characters change during the story. Do the five character areas opposite remain constant or not? For example:

Sheila Birling in *An Inspector Calls*	
The start of Act 1...	As the play develops...
Self-centred and uncaring	Guilty and more thoughtful
Close to her mum and dad	Rebels a little against her parents
Critical of others but defensive of herself	More responsible for her actions
Excitable	More mature
Quite naive	Wiser (about how her actions affect others)

➤ Practise writing paragraphs about how characters change, making use of **connectives** of comparison, time, and **consequence**. Look at this example of a student's revision work about how Sheila changes:

At the start of the play, Sheila is very defensive, 'What do you mean by saying that? You talk as if we were responsible –'. Her rhetorical question, aimed at the Inspector, has an accusatory tone which suggests she doesn't expect to be spoken to in this manner. The use of the phrase 'as if' shows she doesn't consider her family responsible for Eva's death.

> Connective of time and a clear point

> Evidence

> Analysis of language features

As a result of the Inspector's questioning, she begins to accept the consequences of her actions in Act 2: 'And I know I'm to blame – and I'm desperately sorry – but I can't believe – I won't believe – it's simply my fault'. The use of dashes to create pauses in her speech shows how upset she is. This is emphasised by her acceptance of 'blame' and the adverb 'desperately'. However, the repeating negatives ('can't... won't') indicate she's still in a state of denial.

> Connective of consequence and a clear point

> Evidence

> Analysis of sentence structure

> Connective of comparison

Make a paper chain of men and women to represent the characters in your story, and label them with lots of information. Try to include the different things mentioned in the 'Main Characters' section. To develop your skills, include labels about how each character develops on the backs of the paper chain figures.

1. Who are your main characters?

2. What five words would you use to describe each of your main characters?

3. How do your main characters change?

Identifying Your Themes

➤ Start by deciding what the main ideas are in the text you are studying. For example:

DNA
➤ **Morality**
➤ Crime and guilt
➤ Gangs and peer pressure

Lord of the Flies
➤ Fear
➤ Leadership and power
➤ Human nature

An Inspector Calls
➤ Morality
➤ **Class**
➤ Truth and justice

Exploring Your Themes

➤ Think about how your text's themes are shown through character and plot, noting down key quotations. For example:

Lord of the Flies: Leadership and Power

➤ Jack and Ralph struggle for power. Disagreement and difference throughout, especially about fire and shelters vs hunting. ('The two boys faced each other. There was the brilliant world of hunting, tactics, fierce exhilaration, skill; and there was the world of longing and baffled common-sense.')

➤ Jack sees leadership as aggression. Jack's treatment of the choir and his rule of Castle Rock. ('We'll have rules!' he cried excitedly. 'Lots of rules! Then when anyone breaks 'em – ')

➤ Ralph sees leadership as discussion. Early chapters where Ralph calls meetings. ('I'm calling an assembly')

➤ The conch is a symbol of **democracy**. Piggy and Ralph value the conch; it's broken when Piggy is killed. ('I got the conch,' said Piggy, in a hurt voice. 'I got a right to speak.')

➤ The children need a leader. They come when called at the start and always need rules. ('The children gave him the same simple obedience that they had given to the men with the megaphones.')

Analysing Language and Structure

➤ You need to be able to write about how themes are shown through the writer's use of language and structure. Using the themes you've identified (your points) and the key quotations you've found (your evidence), practise analysing how themes are presented. For example:

DNA

One way in which Dennis Kelly presents the theme of control is through John Tate and his banning of the word dead, 'New rule; that word is banned and if anyone says it I'm going to have to, you know, bite their face. Or something.' The pause created by the semi-colon after the word 'rule' and the use of the adjective 'banned' show John Tate takes charge of the gang. He maintains his control through specific threats of violence, with the verb 'bite', and more frightening, unspecific threats: the short sentence makes the vagueness of 'Or something' stand out, so the characters and the audience have to imagine what John could do.

> Clear point about theme, linked to character and event

> Well-chosen quotation with plenty to analyse

> Analysis of sentence structure

> Analysis of language, using technical terms

> Development of analysis

Morality ➤
seeing the difference between good and bad.

Class ➤
social groupings (i.e. upper, middle, lower) based on wealth, education, etc.

Democracy ➤
a form of government controlled by the people that offers equality through voting and elections.

Find a series of objects or pictures to represent the different themes in your text. Write key quotes on small cards to show the characters and events that link to each theme, and tie them to your pictures and objects. To develop your skills, write point, evidence, analysis (PEA) paragraphs on the back of each card, using different colours for your point, your evidence, and your analysis.

1. What are the key themes in your text?

2. Which characters and events link to each of your themes?

3. In your text, which themes create conflict between characters?

Play or Novel?

➤ You need to think about whether your 20th century fiction text is a play or novel, and how this affects the ways in which meaning is conveyed to the audience.

➤ Novelists include detailed descriptions of setting so the reader can fully imagine where the story takes place. However, a play is written to be performed with **dialogue**, so a playwright will use **stage directions** to establish important items (such as furniture) and their location on stage, and how music and lighting should be used to add atmosphere.

32

Settings

➤ A novel will usually have a wider variety of settings to a play (because they can be easily described, whereas a play would need to keep changing the set); however, a play will sometimes make much more specific use of time in order to make it clear how a story is unfolding on stage.

➤ Start by identifying your different settings, where in the text they are used, and key quotations. For example:

Animal Farm

Setting	Chapters	Key Quotations (and notes on features of language and structure)
The fields	Chapters 2, 3, 5, 7	'The grass and the bursting hedges were gilded by the level rays of the sun' (metaphor)
The farmhouse	Chapters 2, 6	'gazing with a kind of awe at the unbelievable luxury' (verb, nouns and adjective)

Dialogue ➤

speech between two or more characters.

Stage direction ➤

information on how a play should look and be performed.

Symbolise ➤

when an object or image represents some other meaning.

Writing About Setting

➤ When exploring setting, think about what it's like, how this has been achieved by the writer, and how it relates to the context. You should also think about how a setting helps us to understand things about character or theme. Look at these revision notes by a student about the opening stage directions from *An Inspector Calls*:

Dining room of a fairly large suburban house, belonging to a fairly prosperous manufacturer. It is a solidly built room, with good solid furniture of the period. A little upstage of centre is a solid but not too large dining room table with a solid set of dining room chairs around it. A few imposing but tasteless pictures and engravings. The general effect is substantial and comfortable and old-fashioned but not cosy and homelike.

The size of the room ('fairly large') indicates the family's wealth and links to the theme of class.

The repeated use of 'solid' furniture **symbolises** the family's confidence and again links to class.

The furniture is 'period' so the audience can recognise the setting as early 20th century.

The dining room setting links to theme of family and shows they are close but also quite formal. The fact it isn't 'cosy' might suggest a lack of love.

The room and its furnishings should show elements of Mr Birling's character (as he is the head of the house). The paintings ('imposing but tasteless') symbolise his desire to show off his wealth, but his lack of sensitivity; he values money over all things.

The room should seem 'comfortable' so when the Inspector arrives he stands out more and seems to clash with the setting.

Important Contexts

➤ Think about the different things that might affect the way in which the story was written and the way in which we receive it. This might include when the story was written, when it is set, the social groupings of the characters, what sort of person the story was written by, etc. For example:

Lord of the Flies: Context
➤ William Golding was a schoolteacher
➤ The novel was published in 1954, soon after the horrors of WW2
➤ The setting is a desert island with no adults
➤ British politics was dominated by ex-public schoolboys
➤ The book presents boys of different class and attitude

 Think about your settings by drawing them, building a mini stage set, or turning them into a map.

1. What are the settings and contexts of your text?
2. How do they tell you things about the story's characters?
3. How do they tell you things about the story's themes?

Who are your main characters and how do they develop?

What are the main settings of the text? What can they tell you about characters?

State an idea, support it with evidence, analyse how features of language or structure have conveyed your idea.

Modern Texts

What are the main themes of your text? How are they shown through character, setting and events?

What key quotations can you find about character, setting and theme?

Have you studied a novel or a play? How does this affect the ways in which character, theme and setting are presented?

1. _DNA_

   'They might even give me money for it, do you think I should ask for money?'
   How does Dennis Kelly develop the character of Cathy?

   [30 marks] + (AO4) [4 marks]

2. _Lord of the Flies_

   Choose one point in the novel where conflict is shown and explain how it is
   presented by the author. **[30 marks] + (AO4) [4 marks]**

3. _Animal Farm_

   'Though not yet full-grown they were huge dogs, and as fierce-looking as wolves.
   They kept close to Napoleon. It was noticed that they wagged their tails to him in
   the same way as the other dogs had been used to do to Mr Jones.'

   How does George Orwell present the theme of power? Refer to the context of
   the novel. **[30 marks] + (AO4) [4 marks]**

4. _An Inspector Calls_

   'But you're partly to blame. Just as your father is.'

   How does J B Priestley present the character of Inspector Goole?

   [30 marks] + (AO4) [4 marks]

5. _Blood Brothers_

   How does Russell use the narrator to explore themes in _Blood Brothers_?

   [30 marks] + (AO4) [4 marks]

6. _The History Boys_

   How does Bennet write about social class and aspiration in _The History Boys_?

   [30 marks] + (AO4) [4 marks]

7. _Never Let Me Go_

   How does Ishiguro use Cathy to explore ideas about what being human
   means in _Never Let Me Go_? **[30 marks] + (AO4) [4 marks]**

8. _Anita and Me_

   How does Syal present Meena's parents in _Anita and Me_?

   [30 marks] + (AO4) [4 marks]

To generate your own questions, choose a character or theme in the text.
Ask yourself how it has been presented through the author's use of language,
structure and form.

Unseen Non-Fiction

pages 4–5
1. Purpose, audience, form.
2. Inform, explain, describe, argue, persuade, instruct, advise, review.
3. Adults, teenagers, your headteacher, governors, MPs/councillors, pensioners, locals, etc.
4. Newspapers, magazines, encyclopaedia entries, adverts, web-pages, letters, reviews, autobiographies, biographies, etc.

pages 6–7
1. Something that can be proven.
2. Something that people think or feel.
3. At the start of paragraphs.
4. To show you fully understand the text.

pages 8–9
1. Verb = a word that describes an action; noun = thing/object word; adjective = a word that describes a noun;
   adverb = a word that describes a verb.
2. Short sentences, lists, exclamations, questions, use of colons, etc.
3. Start, middle, end.

pages 10–11
1. So you know, specifically, what to compare.
2. A point of comparison, a quotation, explanation/analysis.
3. Similarly, however, whereas, on the other hand, in comparison, in contrast, just as, etc.

pages 12–13
1. Longer sentences, more formal writing, old-fashioned or more complex vocabulary.
2. Points, evidence, analysis.
3. Diary and autobiography. Similar = written by the person they're about, so personal, will contain lots of opinions. Difference = diary written at the time, autobiography written later; diary more personal and, unlike an autobiography, not written to be read so may be more honest and contain 'secrets'; autobiography may be more entertaining and descriptive as it's written to be sold.

page 17 Practice Questions
1. TRUE answers are A , B, F and H. One mark for each correct answer given.
2. 7-8 marks (Level 7-9) for a perceptive detailed interpretation of both texts, giving at least four points of comparison (e.g. A is in the city/B in the country; in A the pupils are miserable/in B they are happy; the writer of B respects the teacher/A does not; both schools use corporal punishment) and using appropriate short quotations.
   4-6 marks (Level 4-6) Clear summary of the texts. Some (2 or 3) clear valid comparisons made and some relevant quotations used.
   1-3 marks (Level 1-3) Attempt to summarise the texts. One valid comparison made.

3. 7-8 marks (Level 7-9) Good analysis of the writer's choice of language. A range of appropriate quotations. Sophisticated subject terminology used appropriately.
   4-6 marks (Level 4-6) Clear explanation of the effects of language choices. Relevant quotation. Appropriate subject terminology.
   1-3 marks (level 1-3) Some attempt at discussing language. Attempt to refer to the text. Subject terminology may be used incorrectly.

4. 13-16 marks (Level 8-9) A range of ideas and perspectives compared perceptively throughout. Methods used (e.g. language techniques) to convey those ideas and perspectives analysed. A range of appropriate quotations.
   9-12 marks (Level 6-7) Several ideas and perspectives compared in a clear and relevant way. Methods used to convey ideas and perspectives clearly explained. Relevant quotations from both texts.
   5-6 marks (Level 4-5) Some comparison of ideas and perspectives. Some explanation of methods used. Some reference to at least one text.
   1-4 marks (Level 1-3) A simple answer showing some understanding of at least one text and some awareness of methods used.

Unseen Fiction

pages 18–19
1. So you know, specifically, what type of information you need and where you should retrieve it from.
2. Capital letters to help you spot names of people, places, etc., and numbers to help you spot dates, ages, statistics, etc.
3. Synonyms can help you find sections of the text that relate to the theme you've been given.

pages 20–21
1. Sentence structure = the way punctuation and sentence types have been used to convey information in different ways. Narrative structure = how the whole text has been organised in order to establish and develop ideas.
2. Short sentences, long sentences, lists, dashes, ellipses, exclamations, questions, etc.
3. Start, middle, end.

pages 22–23
1. Character, setting, mood.
2. *What* helps you to establish the idea that has been conveyed, whilst *How* pushes you to analyse the different features of language that have been used to achieve this.
3. Verbs, adjectives, adverbs, simile, metaphor, personifications, images, contrasts, etc.

page 25 Practice Questions

1. One mark each for any four of the following: Miranda goes to boarding school; she lives opposite the Town Hall Annexe; she has a younger sister; she uses the library; she has blonde hair / wears her hair in a pigtail.

2. Level 8–9: a detailed understanding of how the opening is structured and its effect on the reader, for example holding back and building up details about Miranda (from her appearance to her actual name), making the narrator seem increasingly strange and obsessive, and indicating that he will get to know her; well-chosen quotations and perceptive explanations that make good use of inference.
   Level 4–5: clear references to the start, middle and end of the passage, focussing on what we find out about Miranda and some comments about the reader's response to the narrator; several, relevant, well-explained quotations with some inference.

3. Level 8–9: a detailed response to language, with well-chosen quotations that show or suggest the narrator's obsession with Miranda; a range of terminology used to analyse how meaning is conveyed to the reader.
   Level 4–5: a clear understanding of how language is used to make the narrator seem obsessive; several, relevant quotations, with clear explanations and some comments on the effects of specific techniques.

4. Level 8–9: a balanced response, but with clear judgements, analysing how the narrator is presented as romantic and how he is presented as frightening; well-chosen quotations and a range of technical analysis of how meaning is conveyed.
   Level 4–5: a clear response and judgement, but tending to focus more on one side of the argument; several, relevant quotations, with clear explanations and some comments on the effects of specific techniques.

Writing
pages 26–27

1. A series of vivid pictures in their head.
2. Adjective, adverbs, simile, metaphor, personification, images, contrasts, senses, onomatopoeia, alliteration, sibilance, etc.
3. Short sentence to surprise; compound sentences to create contrasts; complex sentences to include lots of detail; lists to build up ideas.

pages 28-29

1. A narrative is a story or account of events. A narrator is someone who tells a story.
2. To describe events that happened before the main action.
3. The main character, who the story is about.

pages 30–31

1. Argue and persuade.
2. A conclusion or summary that gives your final judgement.
3. Connectives of comparison, contrast, and cause/effect.

pages 32–33

1. The audience's opinions.
2. FORESTRY.
3. Facts, Opinions, Rhetorical questions, Empathy and emotive language, Statistics, Triplets, Repetition, You.

pages 34–35

1. For example: ambition, correction, fiction, imagination, nation, operation, pollution, situation, translation, etc.
2. There points out a place; their indicates ownership; they're is an abbreviation of they are.
3. For example: weight (how heavy something is) + wait (to pause).

pages 36–37

1. Simple, compound, complex.
2. Dialogue or sometimes for a first person narrative.
3. Past

pages 38–39

1. Quotation, titles, direct speech.
2. To show the start of a sentence or to indicate a proper noun (name of a person, place or establishment).
3. To indicate abbreviation or ownership.

pages 42–43 Practice Questions
Paper 1 Q1–4 and Paper 2 Q1–4

Marks allocated for how successfully the piece of writing meets the requirements of the task, and for accuracy of spelling, punctuation and grammar.
Level 8–9: convincing and engaging writing throughout; writing fully matched to required purpose, audience and form; sustained use of ambitious vocabulary and a range of techniques; well-structured and fully developed, with complex ideas; varied and inventive structural features, with fluently linked paragraphs; a wide range of punctuation and the full range of sentence structures are used accurately and consistently; complex grammar and spelling are secure.
Level 4–5: clear writing throughout; writing is generally matched to required purpose, audience and form; vocabulary and some techniques chosen successfully for effect; ideas are clearly connected and paragraphs are mostly appropriate with some structural features to keep meaning clear; punctuation and sentences are generally accurate, with some range of structures used for effect; grammar is mostly secure and spelling of familiar, complex words is accurate.

Poetry
pages 44–45

1. Verb = doing word; adjective = a word that describes a noun; adverb = a word that describes a verb.
2. Simile = a comparison using 'like' or 'as'; metaphor = a comparison that's impossible but is written as if it's true.
3. Short sentences, lists, pattern of three, repetition, exclamation, enjambment, etc.

pages 46–47

1. Two
2. Relevance to the question and your confidence in writing about it
3. Refer to the question and sum up your main points.

pages 48–49

1. Themes, Imagery, Form, Structure.
2. How it's conveying the theme.
3. Form = the type of poem and its shape (including number of stanzas, rhyme, line-length, etc).

pages 50–51

1. Themes, imagery, form, structure.
2. Make a clear point, support it with a quotation as evidence, and analyse how the language, form or structure within your quotation gets across the point you made.
3. A traditional form of love poetry, containing 14 lines, 10 syllables per line, and a clear rhyme scheme.

pages 52–53

1. Connectives of comparison.
2. An everyday or slang word/phrase.

page 55 Practice Questions

Q1 and **Q2.**

Level 8–9: a detailed, perceptive and focussed comparison, with a variety of links providing a full exploration of ideas, viewpoints and contexts; well-chosen, precise references; a range of terminology used to analyse the different methods of language, structure and form by which the poets convey meaning.

Level 4–5: a clear, mostly sustained comparison, focussed on the question, with specific links showing a good understanding of ideas, viewpoints and contexts; relevant references and clear explanations of several different ways in which poets use language, structure and form to convey meaning; some use of terminology.

pages 56–57 Practice Questions

Q1.

Level 8–9: a detailed, perceptive and focussed response, presenting a variety of ideas; well-chosen, precise quotations; a range of terminology used to analyse the different methods of language, structure and form by which the poet conveys meaning.

Level 4–5: a clear response, mostly focussed on the question, with a number of ideas showing a good understanding of the poem; relevant quotations and clear explanations of different ways in which the poet uses language, structure and form to convey meaning; some use of terminology.

Q1 Possible Content:

- Short sentence at the start to emphasise shock.
- Use of adjectives 'small feverish' to show concern.
- Use of verb 'knelt' to suggest begging/desperation.
- Repetition of 'shook you' to show terror.
- Contrasting the nice 'blue' of the blanket to the way the 'blue' of the face implies death.
- Rhetorical question to show shock at what she might have to do.
- Simile to show her panic.
- Repetition of intensifier 'so' to show her desperation.
- 'Oh Jesus' suggests surprise and relief, as well as a prayer of thanks.
- Repetition of 'you' and 'your' throughout shows

the importance of the child.

Q2 Possible Content:

- Clear love for the children.
- Both children seem beautiful and tiny.
- Both poets fear for their children's lives.
- One mother seems quite confident in what to do, the other seems unsure.
- Feeling happy and impressed that both children are strong.
- Both use first person – persona of mother.
- Similies used in both, e.g. 'fluttering like flags' and 'like a load of damp laundry'.
- Both use enjambment.

Shakespeare

pages 58–59

1. What they're like and how their character develops.
2. For example: Lady Macbeth – ambitious, controlling, scheming, domineering.
3. For example: unable to control Macbeth's behaviour; mad and unable to rest; full of guilt for what she has done.

pages 60–61

1. For example: *Romeo and Juliet* – love, tragedy, time, fate, family, conflict.
2. For example: *Macbeth* – ambition because it's the driving force for the things that Macbeth and Lady Macbeth do, as well as the way in which the witches trick Macbeth.
3. Where the theme appears, how characters are used to explore it, and how their language links to the theme.

pages 62–63

1. Context = the historical events, attitudes, beliefs and behaviour that affect a piece of writing.
2. For example: *Much Ado About Nothing* – courtly behaviour, traditional expectations of women, attitudes towards illegitimacy and sex before marriage.
3. Traditional = a view of normality based on what has happened in the past.

pages 64–65

1. You need to be more detailed and analytical because you have the text in front of you.
2. Analyse how different features of language and structure in your quotation convey meaning.
3. Saying one thing but actually having the opposite meaning.

pages 66–67

1. For example: the theme of parents and children in *Romeo and Juliet* – Act 1 scene 2 and 3, Act 3 scene 5, Act 4 scene 5, Act 5 scene 3.
2. How features of language, structure and form show the theme.
3. A question asked to make the audience think rather than answer.

pages 69–71: Practice Questions

Part a. (response to an extract).

Level 8–9: a detailed, focussed and cohesive

response; well-chosen, subtle quotations; sustained, perceptive analysis of language, structure and form, making use of a range of terminology to explore the effects on the audience.

Level 4–5: a clear, mostly focussed response; a variety of relevant quotations; clear explanations of how language, structure and form convey meaning, with some terminology, showing a good understanding of the effects on the audience.

Part b. (response to the whole text).

Level 8–9: a personal, focussed and well-developed response; a wide range of points supported by well-chosen references; detailed understanding of the effects of context on the play.

Level 4–5: a relevant, focussed response with some development; some range of points supported by relevant references; clear comments on the effects of context on the play.

Page 69: Possible Content

- Benedick scorns love and people who fall in love.
- He is scornful of Claudio falling in love after saying he wouldn't (which is ironic as Benedick later does the same).
- Benedick sees things to do with being a soldier as manly, and things to do with love as unmanly and foolish.
- Benedick wonders whether he too could fall in love, but decides he won't.
- He doesn't believe his ideal woman exists; he expects a woman to be perfect.
- He makes jokes, such as listing the qualities a woman must have and then saying that he doesn't mind about her hair colour.
- Benedick is quite mischievous: mocking his friends and then hiding from them.

  Elsewhere in the play, Benedick is presented as mostly popular and funny. He is rude (when talking to Beatrice) and likes to be the centre of attention. However, he is more honest about his feelings for her when he finds she loves him back. He shows honour in his willingness to fight Claudio for Beatrice.

Page 70: Possible Content

- In the extract, Macbeth is presented as brave and honourable for his fighting against the Norwegians.
- He is also respected by the other Lords and the King is grateful.
- However, he is also presented as ambitious and untrustworthy in his aside.

  Elsewhere in the play, Macbeth is presented as a man with a conscience (his wish to be a good subject to the King), but easily manipulated by his wife and his ambitions. He becomes paranoid, cruel, and reckless.

Page 71: Possible Content

- In the extract, Lord Capulet feels Juliet is too young to be married.
- He wants Paris to wait for two years because he wants the marriage to last.
- He loves her, more so because she is his only living child, and wants her to have a good life.
- He seems a bit of a romantic and wants Juliet to make her own choices in love.
- He tests Paris by inviting him to look at other girls during the party.

  Elsewhere in the play, Lord Capulet seems violent (his willingness to fight and his reaction to Tybalt at the party) but is wise enough to try to calm the feud with the Montagues after the Prince's orders. He seems a bad father when he suddenly decides to arrange Juliet's marriage. His attitude towards her when she refuses the marriage is cruel. He is upset after her fake death and, after her real death, wants to stop the family feud completely.

The 19th-Century Novel
pages 72–73

1. For example: *The Strange Case of Dr Jekyll and Mr Hyde* – Utterson, Enfield, Dr Jekyll/Mr Hyde.
2. For example: Pip – nice, lacks confidence, aware of lower social status, close to Joe, loves Estella; becomes a gentlemen, grows ashamed of Joe and increasingly selfish, then regrets his behaviour and makes amends, still loves Estella.
3. For example: Rochester is a member of the 19th century upper class, but doesn't meet their social expectations and is willing to marry 'beneath him'; however, he hides his past sins partly to maintain respectability.

pages 74–75

1. For example: settings in *Great Expectations* – Kent marshes, Pip's house and the forge, Satis House, central London.
2. For example: in *Jane Eyre*, Thornfield shows us a lot about Rochester's character, such as his apparent unfriendliness, his dark secrets, his wealth, etc.
3. For example: *In The Strange Case of Dr Jekyll and Mr Hyde*, the setting of Dr Jekyll's house represents his facade of social respectability (the front door) and his actual corrupt nature (the side entrance).

pages 76–77

1. For example: *The Strange Case of Dr Jekyll and Mr Hyde* – reputation and respectability, violence, human nature, science.
2. For example: class in *Great Expectations* links to the differences between Pip and Estella, Pip's feelings of insignificance and his wish to be a gentlemen, his changing attitudes towards Joe, etc.
3. For example: the theme of cruelty in *Jane Eyre* links to attitudes towards the poor and towards children in Victorian society.

page 79 Practice Questions
Q1–3.

Level 8–9: a detailed, perceptive and focussed response, presenting a variety of ideas; well-chosen, precise quotations and references; a range of terminology used to analyse the different methods of language, structure and form by which the writer conveys meaning.

Level 4–5: a clear response, mostly focussed on the question, with a number of ideas showing a good understanding of the text; relevant quotations or references; clear explanations of different ways in which the writer conveys meaning through language, structure and form, with some use of terminology.

Q1 Possible Content:

- Reactions of the witness.

- Physical descriptions of Hyde.
- Descriptions of Hyde's behaviour.
- Hyde's aggressive speech.
- Jekyll's inability to stop changing into Hyde.
- Jekyll's horror at his actions as Hyde.
- The contrast between Jekyll's respectability and Hyde's monstrosity.

Q2 Possible Content:
- Miss Havisham's appearance.
- The setting in which she is placed.
- Her sometimes mysterious dialogue.
- The way she changes when the subject of love appears.
- Her strange behaviour towards Estella.
- When she reveals how she has manipulated Pip and Estella in order to break Pip's heart, and her reaction to his feelings of upset.

Q3 Possible Content:
- Unjustness of Jane's punishment.
- Mr Brocklehurst's language.
- Reactions of witnesses.
- How Jane is treated by the Reeds.
- The harsh conditions at Lowood.
- Jane's punishment at Lowood.
- Rochester's treatment of Jane when it seems that he is due to marry Blanche Ingram.
- The treatment of Bertha Mason.

Modern Texts
pages 80–81
1. For example: *Animal Farm* – Snowball, Napoleon, Boxer, Squealer, Benjamin.
2. For example: Jack in *Lord of the Flies* – aggressive, superior, selfish, instinctive, childish.
3. For example: Jan in *DNA*: loves/needs Phil, wants attention, insecure; as the play develops, we also see a more sensible, caring and moral side to her.

pages 82–83
1. For example: *Lord of the Flies* – power, leadership, human nature, friendship, fear.
2. For example: morality in *An Inspector Calls* – Inspector Goole represents morality, and he challenges the lack of this in the Birling family, managing to make some characters, like Sheila, develop more of a conscience.
3. For example: *Animal Farm* – leadership creates conflict between Snowball and Napoleon; the need to make sacrifices creates conflict between Clover and Molly.

pages 84–85
1. For example: *DNA* – an indeterminate but clearly modern world and the lives of teenagers.
2. For example: *DNA* – the characters can represent any young people in modern society, which is why the characters' names and gender can be changed; each character represents characteristics of, and difficulties faced by, young people.
3. For example: *An Inspector Calls* – the theme of

class and justice link to the social position of the working class at the start of the 20th century.

page 87 Practice Questions
Q1–8.
Level 8–9: a detailed, perceptive and focussed response, presenting a variety of ideas; well-chosen, precise quotations and references; a range of terminology used to analyse the different methods of language, structure and form by which the writer conveys meaning.
Level 4–5: a clear response, mostly focussed on the question, with a number of ideas showing a good understanding of the text; relevant quotations or references; clear explanations of different ways in which the writer conveys meaning through language, structure and form, with some use of terminology.

Q1 Possible Content:
- From the start, Cathy doesn't appear to regret what's happened.
- She seems excited by bad behaviour and is excited by the TV coverage.
- She is selfish and greedy.
- Cathy follows whoever is leader and gains their trust so she becomes more powerful as the play progresses.
- She has a very cruel side to her.
- She finally becomes leader.

Q2 Possible Content:
- The initial fight for leadership between Jack and Ralph.
- Jack's treatment of Piggy at different points in the play.
- The conflict that is caused after the fire goes out.
- The confrontation at Castle Rock.
- The final hunting of Ralph.

Q3 Possible Content:
- Gaining power through respect – Old Major, Snowball, Napoleon.
- Power leads to corruption – the pigs' changing of the Commandments; the final scene.
- Power leads to cruelty – Mr Jones, Napoleon.
- Using violence to keep power – the dogs, the trials.

Q4 Possible Content:
- Mysterious.
- Knowledgeable.
- Confident, demanding and confrontational; not intimidated by the Birlings.
- An upholder of justice and morality.
- A mouthpiece for the rights of working class people.

Q5 Possible Content
- Narrator links scenes.
- Bridge between audience and action.
- Interprets action.
- Knows how things will turn out.
- Talks of fate and superstitions.
- Comments on class differences.

Q6 Possible Content

- Boys all at grammar school trying for Oxford.
- School's aspiration seen as unusual.
- Differences in boys' backgrounds.
- How the boys end up after university.
- Different backgrounds and ambitions of teachers.
- Is education a way of changing class?
- Is aspiration seen as a good thing?

Q7 Possible Content

- Cathy is the narrator and we see the action through her.
- Her true nature is gradually revealed.
- She is curious about her background and what it means.
- The clones imitate human behaviour.
- Seeing through their eyes we might see human behaviour in a new light.
- Clones are seen as dispensable.
- Do they have feelings and emotions like humans?

Q8 Possible Content

- She admires her father and is in awe of him.
- She also admires and loves her mother.
- In some ways they are very traditional but in others not.
- Through them she learns about her cultural background.
- They are different from other parents in the village.
- They might seem idealised and unreal to some readers.

Expectations of spelling, punctuation and grammar for all exam answers.

Level 8–9: spelling and punctuation are consistently accurate; a full range of vocabulary and sentence structures are used to effectively control meaning.

Level 4–5: spelling and punctuation are mostly accurate; a range of vocabulary and sentence structures are used to achieve a general control of meaning.

Index

Acknowledgements

P.11, 12 'Toast' by Nigel Slater (Fourth Estate, 2003). Reprinted by permission of HarperCollins Publishers Ltd © Nigel Slater, 2003.

P.11 Kevin Durant – NBA speech.

P.15 From p.8-9 'Autobiography' by Morrissey (Penguin Classics 2013) Copyright © Whores in Retirement 2011. (Penguin Books Ltd.)

P.25 From *The Collector* by *John Fowles*. Published by Jonathan Cape. Reprinted by permission of The Random House Group Limited.

P.22 From *Growing Rich* by Fay Weldon. Reprinted by permission of HarperCollins Publishers Ltd © Fay Weldon, 1992.

P.48 'Horned Poppy' from *The Book of Blood* by *Vicki Feaver*. Published by *Jonathan Cape*. Reprinted by permission of The Random House Group Limited.

P.53 'Jelly Fish' by Marianne Moore, from *O To Be A Dragon* (Faber and Faber Ltd). Reproduced by permission of Faber and Faber Ltd.

P.53 'Fish' from The *Llama Who Had No Pajama* by Mary Ann Hoberman. Reprinted by permission of The Gina Maccoby Literary Agency © 1959 Mary Ann Hoberman.

P.56 'Daughter' by Ellen Bryant Voigt from *The Forces of Plenty* (W.W. Norton & Company, 1983).

P.57 'Her First Week' From *The Unswept Room by Sharon Olds*. Published by Jonathan Cape. Reprinted by permission of The Random House Group Limited.

P.80, P.82 *Lord of the Flies* by William Golding (Faber and Faber Ltd). Reproduced by permission of Faber and Faber Ltd.

P.81, P.85, P.87 From *An Inspector Calls* by J B Priestley (Heinemann, 1945). (Penguin Books Ltd.)

P.83, 87 DNA © Dennis Kelly 2009. By kind permission of Oberon Books Ltd.

P.84, P.87 *Animal Farm* by George Orwell (Copyright © George Orwell, 1945) (Bill Hamilton as the Literary Executor of the Estate of the Late Sonia Brownell Orwell.)

GCSE Success

AQA

English
Language & Literature

Exam
Practice
Workbook

Complete
Revision & Practice

Ian Kirby
and
Paul Burns

Contents

Read Source A, an extract from 'Auto Da Fay', the autobiography of the novelist Fay Weldon. Published in 2002, this extract describes an earthquake in New Zealand when her mother was still pregnant with Fay.

Source A

When I was three months in the womb, in a period no doubt of nothing happening and nothing happening except a general warm all-pervasive dullness, an earthquake in Napier, New Zealand, had my mother Margaret running from the house with my two-year-old sister Jane in her arms. The year was 1931. My mother was twenty-three. Our house stayed upright but the grammar school opposite and the hospital down the road, both made of brick and not New Zealand's usual wood, collapsed. Everything else seemed made of matchsticks. My mother, in search of my father, one of the town's few doctors, ran past the grammar school and saw arms and legs sticking out of the rubble. But with a small child in your arms, what can you do for others? Everyone else was running too, some one way, some another: the ground was still shaking and changing and whether you were running into more danger or less how could you be sure? But still she ran.

Dr Frank Birkinshaw, my father, was too busy with the injured to take care of his young wife. He was a man of great charm, tall, well built, blue-eyed, adventurous and impetuous – at the time in his mid-thirties. Margaret was small, dark, fastidious and very, very pretty, with high cheekbones, big brown eyes and a gentle manner. The Birkinshaws were recent immigrants from England. He was from the North, had joined the army when he was sixteen, been invalided out of the trenches, and qualified as a doctor in the face of many obstacles. She was a bohemian from the softer South, an intellectual by birth, breeding, and temperament: her father a novelist, her mother a musician. She kept the company of Evelyn Waugh and his gang of friends, she was at home in literary soirées and in fashionable nightclubs, not in this harsh pioneering land. But she was also clever, determined and tough and failing to find my father, she left word for him, and by nightfall she and Jane had taken refuge in the tented city that went up overnight on the hills above Napier. The town was uninhabitable.

My mother was rescued from her makeshift tent by a sheep farmer and his wife, grateful patients of my father. They took her and little Jane to their homestead, where there was, my mother said, mutton for breakfast, mutton for dinner and mutton for tea. She helped around the farm, and cooked and ate the mutton with gratitude. I inherit this gift from her, I daresay, in that I do what is under my nose to be done, without too much lamentation.

Although the ground shook and trembled for weeks after the initial quake, meals continued to be served in the cookhouse, which had a tall brick chimney. My mother lived in fear of it collapsing and killing everyone inside, but no one would listen to her. She was dismissed as an alarmist. She was right, of course. There was another bad shock. 'I felt the trembling begin beneath my feet. I snatched Jane from her cot on the veranda and ran for open space but I was flung to the ground by what seemed a wave of dry land. I saw the hedge flick first one way and then the other. And then I watched the chimney fall into the cookhouse and destroy it. I always knew it would. I had already seen it happen.' As it fell out, dinner had finished just minutes before, and no one was killed, though for a time meals had to be eaten in the open air.

I have not inherited my mother's gift for prophecy: true, as you grow older you may begin to know what is going to happen next, but this can be put down to experience, not second sight. It is not a happy gift to have: because of it, for one thing, my mother never learned to drive, seeing too many scenarios of disaster ahead for comfort, too conscious of what might be going on over the brow of the hill. My father was very different: he was over-confident: he saw to the pleasures of the here-and-now and let the future go hang. I was born more like him than her, in this respect. She prophesied that it would land us both in trouble, and she was right.

Read Source B, an extract from an essay 'Thoughts On Cheapness and My Aunt Charlotte', published in 1898 by the novelist H.G. Wells. In this extract, he describes the amount of good ornaments and furniture that his aunt used to keep, and wonders whether it's better to buy cheap things that will break rather than out-live you.

Source B

All my Aunt Charlotte's furniture was thoroughly good, and most of it extremely uncomfortable; there was not a thing for a little boy to break and escape damnation in the household. Her china was the only thing with a touch of beauty in it – at least I remember nothing else – and each of her blessed plates was worth the happiness of a mortal for days together. I learned the value of thoroughly good things only too early. I knew the equivalent of a teacup to the very last scowl, and I have hated good, handsome property ever since. For my part I love cheap things, trashy things, things made of the commonest rubbish that money can possibly buy; things as vulgar as primroses, and as transitory as a morning's frost.

Think of all the advantages of a cheap possession – cheap and nasty, if you will – compared with some valuable substitute. Suppose you need this or that. "Get a good one," advises Aunt Charlotte; "one that will last." You do – and it does last. It lasts like a family curse. These great plain valuable things, as plain as good women, as complacently assured of their intrinsic worth – who does not know them? My Aunt Charlotte scarcely had a new thing in her life. Her mahogany was avuncular; her china remotely ancestral; her feather beds and her bedsteads! – they were haunted; the births, marriages, and deaths associated with the best one was the history of our race for three generations. There was more in her house than the tombstone rectitude of the chair-backs to remind me of the graveyard. I can still remember the sombre aisles of that house, the vault-like shadows, the magnificent window curtains that blotted out the windows. Life was too trivial for such things. She never knew she tired of them, but she did. That was the secret of her temper, I think; they engendered her sombre Calvinism, her perception of the trashy quality of human life. The pretence that they were the accessories to human life was too transparent. We were the accessories; we minded them for a little while, and then we passed away. They wore us out and cast us aside. We were the changing scenery; they were the actors who played on through the piece. It was even so with clothing. We buried my other maternal aunt – Aunt Adelaide – and wept, and partly forgot her; but her wonderful silk dresses – they would stand alone – still went rustling cheerfully about an ephemeral world.

All that offended my sense of proportion, my feeling of what is due to human life, even when I was a little boy. I want things of my own, things I can break without breaking my heart; and, since one can live but once, I want some change in my life – to have this kind of thing and then that. I never valued Aunt Charlotte's good old things until I sold them. They sold remarkably well: those chairs like nether millstones for the grinding away of men; the fragile china – an incessant anxiety until accident broke it, and the spell of it at the same time; those silver spoons, by virtue of which Aunt Charlotte went in fear of burglary for six-and-fifty years; the bed from which I alone of all my kindred had escaped; the wonderful old, erect, high-shouldered, silver-faced clock.

For more help on this topic, see Letts GCSE English Revision Guide pages 4–14.

1 Re-read the first paragraph of Source A. Choose four of the following statements that are true:

a) Fay was two years old when the earthquake took place. ☐

b) Fay's mother stopped to help everyone that she could. ☐

c) The earthquake took place in the city of Napier. ☐

d) Fay doesn't have any brothers or sisters. ☐

e) Fay's mother was 23 years old when the earthquake took place. ☐

f) Fay's mother's name is Margaret. ☐

g) The grammar school didn't collapse during the earthquake because it was brick-built. ☐

h) Fay's father was the local doctor. ☐ (4 marks)

2 You need to refer to Source A and Source B for this question. Write a summary of the differences between Fay's mother and Aunt Charlotte. (8 marks)

....

....

....

....

....

....

....

....

....

3 Look again at the first paragraph of Source B. In this paragraph, how does Wells use language to convey his preference for cheap things over quality things?
(Write your answer on a separate piece of paper.) (12 marks)

4 Referring to Source A and Source B, compare how the two writers convey their different feelings about members of their family. In your answer you should:

➤ compare their different feelings

➤ compare the methods they use to convey their different feelings

➤ support your ideas with quotations from both texts. (16 marks)

(Write your answer on a separate piece of paper.)

Read Source C, an article from *The Guardian* newspaper about kayaking in Australia. Written by Beverley Fearis, it was published in 2014.

Source C

Melbourne in the moonlight: a nighttime kayak tour   (Beverley Fearis, The Guardian, Friday 4 April 2014)

One by one, balls of flames shot up from the towers like mini-infernos, lighting up the city skyline and casting a warm orange glow across the water below. We could hear the mighty whoosh each time the flames rose, followed by a hum of appreciation from the watching crowds lining the riverbank. The nightly fireball display in front of the Crown Casino has become a key feature of Melbourne's night scene, and we had the best seats in the house. Only thing was, we couldn't keep them still. That's the trouble with kayaks.

That morning we had cycled along the bank of the Yarra river, dodging office workers with their iPods and lattes, admiring the architecture and soaking up the city vibe. But now we were seeing Melbourne's hub from a whole different perspective – on a Moonlight Kayak tour, one of the city's more unusual sightseeing experiences. Under cover of darkness, we paddled silently up the Yarra like secret agents, passing under the bridges unseen. It was magical.

We had met at 7pm at Shed 2 of Victoria Harbour in the city's Docklands, like a smaller version of London's Docklands but catching up fast. Kent, our forever smiling (and ridiculously handsome) guide had introduced us to our ride, a two-seater fibreglass SeaBear sea kayak, and given us a quick but thorough briefing – life jackets, steering, paddling.

It was still light as we paddled off, and the low sun was glinting off the brilliant white super yachts lined up along the pontoons. At first, we stuck to the edge of the marina, getting used to our paddles and synchronising our strokes. The going was every bit as easy as Kent had promised. But then we changed direction and suddenly felt the force of the wind whipping across the water.

Warren, my fiancé, in the back, was in charge of steering with a foot pedal, but despite his best efforts we were being pushed towards the underside of a jetty. We had to use our paddles to help make the turn, really putting our backs into it to keep our distance. That was our only hairy moment, though, and we soon caught up with the others, in a sheltered corner of the marina.

Kent tied our kayaks to the jetty and left us chatting with our fellow urban adventurers. He returned a few minutes later with five portions of fish and chips, which we ate bobbing about in our kayaks, dipping our chips into the tartare sauce. Kent told us how he'd moved to Melbourne from Toronto for a marketing job but got sick of the corporate world. A keen kayaker, he'd come up with the idea of the Yarra tours. He does daytime trips too, but the moonlight tour has been the winner. "I think it's the fish and chips," he said, and to be fair they were a big part of the appeal.

Energy levels up, we headed off again, out into the mouth of the marina and past the Star Observation Wheel, Melbourne's answer to the London Eye. It opened in 2008 but closed 40 days later because of major structural defects (it had cracked in the heat). Dismantled and completely rebuilt, it opened again last December. At dusk it lights up in pretty neon colours.

As the sun set, we passed under the enormous Bolte Bridge, with its distinctive twin giant towers (purely aesthetic, Kent told us), then made a sharp left turn to head up the Yarra and into the heart of the city. The wind was in our favour now, so the paddling was easy and at times we let our blades rest and drifted along peacefully, taking it all in. Dusk turned to night and lights on the skyscrapers started to twinkle. As we cruised, Kent pointed out the landmarks, including the Eureka Skydeck, Melbourne's tallest highrise, named after a bloody rebellion during Victoria's 1854 gold rush. Next came the Webb Bridge, with its distinctive futuristic web tunnel for cyclists and pedestrians; and the Sandridge Bridge, with its large metal sculptures entitled The Travellers, representing the immigrants who arrived by train over the bridge from Station Pier. We slipped under the eerie undersides of these famous bridges, paddling through their shadowy arches, some of which were low enough to touch.

I had expected that we would be dodging pleasure cruisers and restaurant boats, waving to people in other boats (like you do when you're a tourist on water), but we had the river completely to ourselves. On either side of us the city night scene was hotting up, restaurants and bars buzzing, and here we were, on our moonlight urban kayak adventure, floating gently through the middle of it, trailing our fingers in the warm water, seeing it all, but unseen, from a vantage point like no other.

For more help on this topic, see Letts GCSE English Revision Guide pages 4–14.

Read Source D, a letter written by the novelist Charles Dickens in 1839 to his friend Thomas Mitton. Living in Exeter, Dickens writes to tell his friend about a cottage that he has decided to rent for his parents.

Source D

New London Inn, Exeter
Wednesday Morning, March 6th, 1839.

Dear Tom,

Perhaps you have heard from Kate that I succeeded yesterday in the very first walk, and took a cottage at a place called Alphington, one mile from Exeter, which contains, on the ground-floor, a good parlour and kitchen, and above, a full-sized country drawing-room and three bedrooms; in the yard behind, coal-holes, fowl-houses, and meat-safes out of number; in the kitchen, a neat little range; in the other rooms, good stoves and cupboards; and all for twenty pounds a year, taxes included. There is a good garden at the side well stocked with cabbages, beans, onions, celery, and some flowers. The stock belonging to the landlady (who lives in the adjoining cottage), there was some question whether she was not entitled to half the produce, but I settled the point by paying five shillings, and becoming absolute master of the whole!

I do assure you that I am charmed with the place and the beauty of the country round about, though I have not seen it under very favourable circumstances, for it snowed when I was there this morning, and blew bitterly from the east yesterday. It is really delightful, and when the house is to rights and the furniture all in, I shall be quite sorry to leave it. I have had some few things second-hand, but I take it seventy pounds will be the mark, even taking this into consideration. I include in that estimate glass and crockery, garden tools, and such like little things. There is a spare bedroom of course. That I have furnished too.

I am on terms of the closest intimacy with Mrs. Samuell, the landlady, and her brother and sister-in-law, who have a little farm hard by. They are capital specimens of country folks, and I really think the old woman herself will be a great comfort to my mother. Coals are dear just now—twenty-six shillings a ton. They found me a boy to go two miles out and back again to order some this morning. I was debating in my mind whether I should give him eighteenpence or two shillings, when his fee was announced—twopence!

The house is on the high road to Plymouth, and, though in the very heart of Devonshire, there is as much long-stage and posting life as you would find in Piccadilly. The situation is charming. Meadows in front, an orchard running parallel to the garden hedge, richly-wooded hills closing in the prospect behind, and, away to the left, before a splendid view of the hill on which Exeter is situated, the cathedral towers rising up into the sky in the most picturesque manner possible. I don't think I ever saw so cheerful or pleasant a spot. The drawing-room is nearly, if not quite, as large as the outer room of my old chambers in Furnival's Inn. The paint and paper are new, and the place clean as the utmost excess of snowy cleanliness can be.

You will have heard perhaps that I wrote to my mother to come down to-morrow. There are so many things she can make comfortable at a much less expense than I could, that I thought it best. If I had not, I could not have returned on Monday, which I now hope to do, and to be in town at half-past eight.

Will you tell my father that if he could devise any means of bringing him down, I think it would be a great thing for him to have Dash, if it be only to keep down the trampers and beggars.

1 Re-read the second and third paragraphs of Source C. Choose four of the following statements that are true:

a) Fearis dislikes the city of Melbourne. ☐

b) Moonlight kayaking is quite unusual. ☐

c) Fearis enjoyed her kayaking experience. ☐

d) The guide was stern and miserable. ☐

e) They met at 7am before the sun came up. ☐

f) They all met up at Victoria Harbour. ☐

g) The kayaks were made from fibreglass. ☐

h) Fearis was scared as she didn't know what she was doing. ☐ (4 marks)

2 Looking at the sixth paragraph of Source C, summarise Kent's reasons for setting up the moonlight kayaking tours. (4 marks)

....

....

....

....

....

....

3 Looking at the fourth paragraph of Source D, summarise what we are told about the cottage's setting in your own words. (4 marks)

....

....

....

....

4 Refer to the first two paragraphs of Source D. How does Dickens use language to convey his enthusiasm for the cottage he has rented for his parents? (12 marks)
(Write your answer on a separate piece of paper.)

5 Referring to Source C and Source D, compare how the two writers convey their different feelings about people and places. In your answer you should:
➤ compare their different feelings
➤ compare the methods they use to convey their different feelings
➤ support your ideas with quotations from both texts. (16 marks)
(Write your answer on a separate piece of paper.)

For more help on this topic, see Letts GCSE English Revision Guide pages 4–14.

Source A is an extract from the opening chapter of 'The Falls', a novel by Joyce Carol Oates that was published in 2004. In this section, the gatekeeper who runs the tourist tollbooth for Niagara Falls sees a young man running towards the bridge.

Source A

By this time the gatekeeper had decided to leave his tollbooth to follow the agitated man. Calling, "Mister! Hey mister!"—"Mister, wait!" He'd had experience with suicides in the past. More times than he wished to remember. He was a thirty-year veteran of The Falls tourist trade. He was in his early sixties, couldn't keep up with the younger man. Pleading, "Mister! Don't! God damn I'm begging you: *don't!*"

He should have dialled his emergency number, back in the tollbooth. Now it was too late to turn back.

Once on Goat Island the younger man didn't pause by the railing to gaze across the river at the Canadian shore, nor did he pause to contemplate the raging, tumultuous scene, as any normal tourist would do. He didn't pause even to wipe his streaming face, or brush his straggly hair out of his eyes. *Under the spell of The Falls. Nobody mortal was going to stop him.*

But you have to interfere, or try. Can't let a man – or a woman – commit suicide, the unforgiveable sin, before your staring eyes.

The gatekeeper, short of breath, light-headed, limped after the younger man shouting at him as he made his unerring way to the southern tip of the little island, Terrapin Point, above the Horseshoe Falls. The most treacherous corner of Goat Island, as it was the most beautiful and enthralling. Here the rapids go into a frenzy. White frothy churning water shooting up fifteen feet into the air. Hardly any visibility. The chaos of a nightmare. The Horseshoe Falls is a gigantic cataract a half-mile long at its crest, three thousand tons of water pouring over the Gorge each second. The air roars, shakes. The ground beneath your feet shakes. As if the very earth is beginning to come apart, disintegrate into particles, down to its molten centre. As if time has ceased. Time has exploded. As if you've come too near to the radiant, thrumming, mad heart of all being. Here, your veins, arteries, the minute precision and perfection of your nerves will be unstrung in an instant. Your brain, in which you reside, that one-of-a-kind repository of *you*, will be pounded into its chemical components: brain cells, molecules, atoms. Every shadow and echo of every memory erased.

Maybe that's the promise of The Falls? The secret?

Like we're sick of ourselves. Mankind. This is the way out, only a few have the vision.

Thirty yards from the younger man, the gatekeeper saw him place one foot on the lowest rung of the railing. A tentative foot, on the slippery wrought iron. But the man's hands gripped the top rung, both fists, tight,

"Don't do it! Mister! God damn—"

The gatekeeper's words were drowned out by The Falls. Flung back into his face like cold spit.

Near to collapsing, himself. This would be his last summer at Goat Island. His heart hurt, pounding to send oxygen to his stunned brain. And his lungs hurt, not only the stinging spray of the river but the strange metallic taste of the air of the industrial city sprawling east and north of The Falls, in which the gatekeeper had lived all his life. *You wear out. You see too much. Every breath hurts.*

The gatekeeper would afterward swear he'd seen the younger man make a gesture of farewell in the instant before he jumped: a mock salute, a salute of defiance, as a bright brash schoolboy might make to an elder, to provoke; yet a sincere farewell too, as you might make to a stranger, a witness to whom you mean no harm, whom you wish to absolve of the slightest shred of guilt he might feel, for allowing you to die when he might have saved you.

And in the next instant the young man, who'd been commandeering the gatekeeper's exclusive attention, was simply – gone.

In a heartbeat, gone. Over the Horseshoe Falls.

1 Look at the first paragraph. List four things about the gatekeeper. (4 marks)

....

....

....

....

2 Referring to the fifth paragraph, how has the writer used language to describe Niagara Falls? (8 marks)
(Write your answer on a separate piece of paper.)

3 You now need to think about the whole of the extract. This text is from the opening chapter of a novel. How has the writer structured the text to interest you as a reader?
You could write about:
➤ what the writer focused your attention on at the beginning
➤ how and why the writer alters this focus as the extract develops
➤ any other structural features that interest you. (8 marks)
(Write your answer on a separate piece of paper.)

4 A student, having read this extract said: 'The writer makes you feel so sorry for the old gatekeeper. He's desperate to stop the man but is totally helpless himself.' To what extent do you agree?
In your response, you should:
➤ write about your own impression of the gatekeeper
➤ evaluate how the writer has created these impressions
➤ support your opinions with quotations from the text. (20 marks)
(Write your answer on a separate piece of paper.)

For more help on this topic, see Letts GCSE English Revision Guide pages 18–24.

Source B is an extract from the opening pages of 'Brokeback Mountain', a short story written by Annie Proulx in 1997. In this section, two young cowboys are introduced to each other as they take a job for the summer.

Source B

They were raised on small, poor ranches in opposite corners of the state, Jack Twist in Lightning Flat up on the Montana border, Ennis del Mar from around Sage, near the Utah line, both high school dropout country boys with no prospects, brought up to hard work and privation, both rough-mannered, rough-spoken, inured to the stoic life. Ennis, reared by his older brother and sister after their parents drove off the only curve on Dead Horse Road leaving them twenty-four dollars in cash and a two-mortgage ranch, applied at age fourteen for a hardship license that let him make the hour-long trip from the ranch to the high school. The pickup was old, no heater, one windshield wiper and bad tires; when the transmission went there was no money to fix it. He had wanted to be a sophomore, felt the word carried a kind of distinction, but the truck broke down short of it, pitching him directly into ranch work.

In 1963 when he met Jack Twist, Ennis was engaged to Alma Beers. Both Jack and Ennis claimed to be saving money for a small spread; in Ennis's case that meant a tobacco can with two five-dollar bills inside. That spring, hungry for any job, each had signed up with Farm and Ranch Employment – they came together on paper as herder and camp tender for the same sheep operation north of Signal. The summer range lay above the tree line on Forest Service land on Brokeback Mountain. It would be Jack Twist's second summer on the mountain, Ennis's first. Neither of them was twenty.

They shook hands in the choky little trailer office in front of a table littered with scribbled papers, a Bakelite ashtray brimming with stubs. The venetian blinds hung askew and admitted a triangle of white light, the shadow of the foreman's hand moving into it. Joe Aguirre, wavy hair the color of cigarette ash and parted down the middle, gave them his point of view.

"Forest Service got designated campsites on the allotments. Them camps can be a couple a miles from where we pasture the sheep. Bad predator loss, nobody near lookin after em at night. What I want, camp tender in the main camp where the Forest Service says, but the HERDER" – pointing at Jack with a chop of his hand – "pitch a pup tent on the q.t. with the sheep, out a sight, and he's goin a SLEEP there. Eat supper, breakfast in camp, but SLEEP WITH THE SHEEP, hundred percent, NO FIRE, don't leave NO SIGN. Roll up that tent every mornin case Forest Service snoops around. Got the dogs, your .30-.30, sleep there. Last summer had goddamn near twenty-five percent loss. I don't want that again. YOU," he said to Ennis, taking in the ragged hair, the big nicked hands, the jeans torn, button-gaping shirt, "Fridays twelve noon be down at the bridge with your next week list and mules. Somebody with supplies'll be there in a pickup." He didn't ask if Ennis had a watch but took a cheap round ticker on a braided cord from a box on a high shelf, wound and set it, tossed it to him as if he weren't worth the reach. "TOMORROW MORNIN we'll truck you up the jump-off." Pair of deuces going nowhere.

They found a bar and drank beer through the afternoon, Jack telling Ennis about a lightning storm on the mountain the year before that killed forty-two sheep, the peculiar stink of them and the way they bloated, the need for plenty of whiskey up there. He had shot an eagle, he said, turned his head to show the tail feather in his hatband. At first glance Jack seemed fair enough with his curly hair and quick laugh, but for a small man he carried some weight in the haunch and his smile disclosed buckteeth, not pronounced enough to let him eat popcorn out of the neck of a jug, but noticeable. He was infatuated with the rodeo life and fastened his belt with a minor bull-riding buckle, but his boots were worn to the quick, holed beyond repair and he was crazy to be somewhere, anywhere else than Lightning Flat.

Ennis, high-arched nose and narrow face, was scruffy and a little cave-chested, balanced a small torso on long, caliper legs, possessed a muscular and supple body made for the horse and for fighting. His reflexes were uncommonly quick and he was farsighted enough to dislike reading anything except Hamley's saddle catalog.

1 Look at the first paragraph. List four things about Ennis del Mar. (4 marks)

....

....

....

....

2 Referring to paragraphs two, five, and six, how has the writer used language to describe Jack and Ennis? (8 marks)
(Write your answer on a separate piece of paper.)

3 You now need to think about the whole of the extract. This text is from the opening pages of a short story. How has the writer structured the text to interest you as a reader?
You could write about:
➤ what the writer focused your attention on at the beginning
➤ how and why the writer alters this focus as the extract develops
➤ any other structural features that interest you. (8 marks)
(Write your answer on a separate piece of paper.)

4 A student, having read paragraphs three and four of the extract said: 'The writer quickly builds up a strong impression of the boss, Joe Aguirre.' To what extent do you agree?
In your response, you should:
➤ write about your own impression of Joe Aguirre
➤ evaluate how the writer has created these impressions
➤ support your opinions with quotations from the text. (20 marks)
(Write your answer on a separate piece of paper.)

For more help on this topic, see Letts GCSE English Revision Guide pages 18–24.

Source C is an extract from Chapter Two of Bram Stoker's 1897 novel, 'Dracula'. In this section, Jonathan Harker arrives at Count Dracula's sinister castle.

Source C

JONATHAN HARKER'S JOURNAL (continued)

5 May. I must have been asleep, for certainly if I had been fully awake I must have noticed the approach of such a remarkable place. In the gloom the courtyard looked of considerable size, and as several dark ways led from it under great round arches, it perhaps seemed bigger than it really is. I have not yet been able to see it by daylight.

When the calèche stopped, the driver jumped down and held out his hand to assist me to alight. Again I could not but notice his prodigious strength. His hand actually seemed like a steel vice that could have crushed mine if he had chosen. Then he took out my traps, and placed them on the ground beside me as I stood close to a great door, old and studded with large iron nails, and set in a projecting doorway of massive stone. I could see even in the dim light that the stone was massively carved, but that the carving had been much worn by time and weather. As I stood, the driver jumped again into his seat and shook the reins; the horses started forward, and trap and all disappeared down one of the dark openings.

I stood in silence where I was, for I did not know what to do. Of bell or knocker there was no sign; through these frowning walls and dark window openings it was not likely that my voice could penetrate. The time I waited seemed endless, and I felt doubts and fears crowding upon me. What sort of place had I come to, and among what kind of people? What sort of grim adventure was it on which I had embarked? Was this a customary incident in the life of a solicitor's clerk sent out to explain the purchase of a London estate to a foreigner? Solicitor's clerk! Mina would not like that. Solicitor – for just before leaving London I got word that my examination was successful; and I am now a full-blown solicitor! I began to rub my eyes and pinch myself to see if I were awake. It all seemed like a horrible nightmare to me, and I expected that I should suddenly awake, and find myself at home, with the dawn struggling in through the windows, as I had now and again felt in the morning after a day of overwork. But my flesh answered the pinching test, and my eyes were not to be deceived. I was indeed awake and among the Carpathians. All I could do now was to be patient, and to wait the coming of the morning.

Just as I had come to this conclusion I heard a heavy step approaching behind the great door, and saw through the chinks the gleam of a coming light. Then there was the sound of rattling chains and the clanking of massive bolts drawn back. A key was turned with the loud grating noise of long disuse, and the great door swung back.

1 Re-read the first two paragraphs. List four facts about the castle. (4 mark)

....

....

....

....

2 In the second paragraph, how does the writer use language to make the castle sound large and old? Support your views with detailed reference to the text.

You could include the writer's choice of:

➤ words and phrases

➤ language features and techniques

➤ sentence forms (8 marks)

(Write your answer on a separate piece of paper.)

3 In this extract how has the writer structured the text to engage the reader?

You could write about:

➤ how the writer focuses your attention at the beginning

➤ how and why the writer changes this focus

➤ any other structural features that interest you. (8 marks)

(Write your answer on a separate piece of paper.)

4 How does the writer use the narrator, Jonathan Harker and his experiences to involve the reader in his story?

In your response you should:

➤ write about your impressions of Harker and his experiences

➤ evaluate how the writer has created those impressions

➤ support your opinions with quotations from the text. (20 marks)

(Write your answer on a separate piece of paper.)

For more help on this topic, see Letts GCSE English Revision Guide pages 18–24.

Source D is an extract from 'The Terror Of The Blue-John Gap', a short story written by Arthur Conan Doyle in 1910. In this section, the narrator, Dr James Hardcastle, gets lost whilst exploring a disused mine.

Source D

And now I come to the point where I met with such sudden and desperate disaster. A stream, some twenty feet broad, ran across my path, and I walked for some little distance along the bank to find a spot where I could cross dry-shod. Finally, I came to a place where a single flat boulder lay near the centre, which I could reach in a stride. As it chanced, however, the rock had been cut away and made top-heavy by the rush of the stream, so that it tilted over as I landed on it and shot me into the ice-cold water. My candle went out, and I found myself floundering about in utter and absolute darkness.

I staggered to my feet again, more amused than alarmed by my adventure. The candle had fallen from my hand, and was lost in the stream, but I had two others in my pocket, so that it was of no importance. I got one of them ready, and drew out my box of matches to light it. Only then did I realize my position. The box had been soaked in my fall into the river. It was impossible to strike the matches.

A cold hand seemed to close round my heart as I realized my position. The darkness was opaque and horrible. It was so utter, one put one's hand up to one's face as if to press off something solid. I stood still, and by an effort I steadied myself. I tried to reconstruct in my mind a map of the floor of the cavern as I had last seen it. Alas! the bearings which had impressed themselves upon my mind were high on the wall, and not to be found by touch. Still, I remembered in a general way how the sides were situated, and I hoped that by groping my way along them I should at last come to the opening of the Roman tunnel. Moving very slowly, and continually striking against the rocks, I set out on this desperate quest.

But I very soon realized how impossible it was. In that black, velvety darkness one lost all one's bearings in an instant. Before I had made a dozen paces, I was utterly bewildered as to my whereabouts. The rippling of the stream, which was the one sound audible, showed me where it lay, but the moment that I left its bank I was utterly lost. The idea of finding my way back in absolute darkness through that limestone labyrinth was clearly an impossible one.

I sat down upon a boulder and reflected upon my unfortunate plight. I had not told anyone that I proposed to come to the Blue John mine, and it was unlikely that a search party would come after me. Therefore I must trust to my own resources to get clear of the danger. There was only one hope, and that was that the matches might dry. When I fell into the river, only half of me had got thoroughly wet. My left shoulder had remained above the water. I took the box of matches, therefore, and put it into my left armpit. The moist air of the cavern might possibly be counteracted by the heat of my body, but even so, I knew that I could not hope to get a light for many hours. Meanwhile there was nothing for it but to wait. Gradually, lulled by the monotonous gurgle of the stream, and by the absolute darkness, I sank into an uneasy slumber.

How long this lasted I cannot say. It may have been for an hour, it may have been for several. Suddenly I sat up on my rock couch, with every nerve thrilling and every sense acutely on the alert. Beyond all doubt I had heard a sound - some sound very distinct from the gurgling of the waters. It had passed, but the reverberation of it still lingered in my ear. Was it a search party? They would most certainly have shouted, and vague as this sound was which had wakened me, it was very distinct from the human voice. I sat palpitating and hardly daring to breathe. There it was again! And again! Now it had become continuous. It was a tread - yes, surely it was the tread of some living creature. But what a tread it was! It gave one the impression of enormous weight carried upon sponge-like feet, which gave forth a muffled but ear-filling sound. The darkness was as complete as ever, but the tread was regular and decisive. And it was coming beyond all question in my direction.

1 From the first paragraph, identify a phrase that suggests something bad is going to happen.   (1 mark)

2 From the first paragraph, identify a phrase that explains why the rock 'tilted over'.   (1 mark)

3 From the second paragraph, give two ways that Hardcastle does not seem bothered by what has happened. Use your own words or quotations from the text.   (2 marks)

4 Look at the third and fourth paragraphs.
How does the writer use language to show Hardcastle's different thoughts and feelings?
You could include the writer's choice of:
➤ words and phrases
➤ language features and techniques
➤ sentence forms   (8 marks)
(Write your answer on a separate piece of paper.)

5 Look at the whole text. How has the writer structured the text to establish an unsettling atmosphere?
You could write about:
➤ how the writer focuses your attention at the beginning
➤ how and why the writer changes this focus
➤ any other structural features that interest you.   (8 marks)
(Write your answer on a separate piece of paper.)

6 A student, having read this extract said, 'the writer succeeds in creating a sense of mystery and fear, making you worried about the narrator and desperate to find out what happens next.' To what extent do you agree?
In your response you should:
➤ write about your impressions of Harker and his experiences
➤ evaluate how the writer has created those impressions
➤ support your opinions with quotations from the text   (20 marks)
(Write your answer on a separate piece of paper.)

For more help on this topic, see Letts GCSE English Revision Guide pages 18–24.

Writing: Starter Questions

(Write your answers to these questions on a separate piece of paper.)

1 Homophones

Insert the correct word in each of the following sentences:

a) They're/there/their

I opened the door but nobody was ….

The dogs had all finished …. breakfasts.

….. coming for tea tonight.

b) To/two/too

There are … many people in this class.

I have …. sisters and a brother.

I want …go home.

c) Write/right

I did it because I thought it was the …. thing to do.

I will … a letter to the paper about it. (8 marks)

2 Word endings

Write down the correct plural forms of the following words:

a) Woman

b) Key

c) Jury

d) Sheep

e) Baby

f) Witch (6 marks)

3 Sentences

What sort of sentences are the following?

a) I got up and left.

b) Although I could not see anyone, I felt a strange presence.

c) I ate the banana. (3 marks)

4 Apostrophes

Insert the apostrophes correctly in these sentences:

a) Shes going to be a star one day.

b) I cant take it anymore.

c) We all love Marcos pizzas.

d) The childrens coats were hanging up.

e) The cats tails are black.

f) Marys gone to Paris. (6 marks)

5 Tenses

Choose the correct word from the alternatives.

a) I did/done my homework yesterday.

b) I give/gave it in this morning.

c) She carried/carryed two shopping bags.

d) He's gonna/going to pass the exam.

e) They have eaten/ate their dinner.

f) She has got/gotten three stars. (6 marks)

Writing to Narrate

(Write your answers to these questions on a separate piece of paper.)

1 Write the opening part of a story that is set in an alien planet.

(24 marks for content and organisation / 16 marks for technical accuracy)

2 Write a personal anecdote about an exciting day out.

(24 marks for content and organisation / 16 marks for technical accuracy)

3 Write the opening part of a story that takes place on a desert island.

(24 marks for content and organisation / 16 marks for technical accuracy)

4 Write the opening part of a story that uses the genre of detective fiction.

(24 marks for content and organisation / 16 marks for technical accuracy)

5 Write a story that begins: ' Suddenly everything changed'.

(24 marks for content and organisation / 16 marks for technical accuracy)

6 Write a story that ends with the words: 'I looked at what I had done and smiled'.

(24 marks for content and organisation / 16 marks for technical accuracy)

7 Write about something that happened when you were very young.

(24 marks for content and organisation / 16 marks for technical accuracy)

8 Write the opening part of a horror story.

(24 marks for content and organisation / 16 marks for technical accuracy)

For more help on this topic, see Letts GCSE English Revision Guide pages 26–41.

Writing to Describe

(Write your answers to these questions on a separate piece of paper.)

1 Write a description using contrasts and the theme 'City and Countryside'.

(24 marks for content and organisation / 16 marks for technical accuracy)

2 Write a description using contrasts and the theme 'Day and Night'.

(24 marks for content and organisation / 16 marks for technical accuracy)

3 Imagine your dream house. Write a description that takes your reader on a tour of the property.

(24 marks for content and organisation / 16 marks for technical accuracy)

4 Write a description inspired by this image of a strange landscape.

(24 marks for content and organisation / 16 marks for technical accuracy)

5 Write a description that uses the theme of 'Extreme Weather'.

(24 marks for content and organisation / 16 marks for technical accuracy)

6 Describe a person you have met recently.

(24 marks for content and organisation / 16 marks for technical accuracy)

7 Describe a busy street in both summer and winter.

(24 marks for content and organisation / 16 marks for technical accuracy)

8 Write a description inspired by this image from a storm.

(24 marks for content and organisation / 16 marks for technical accuracy)

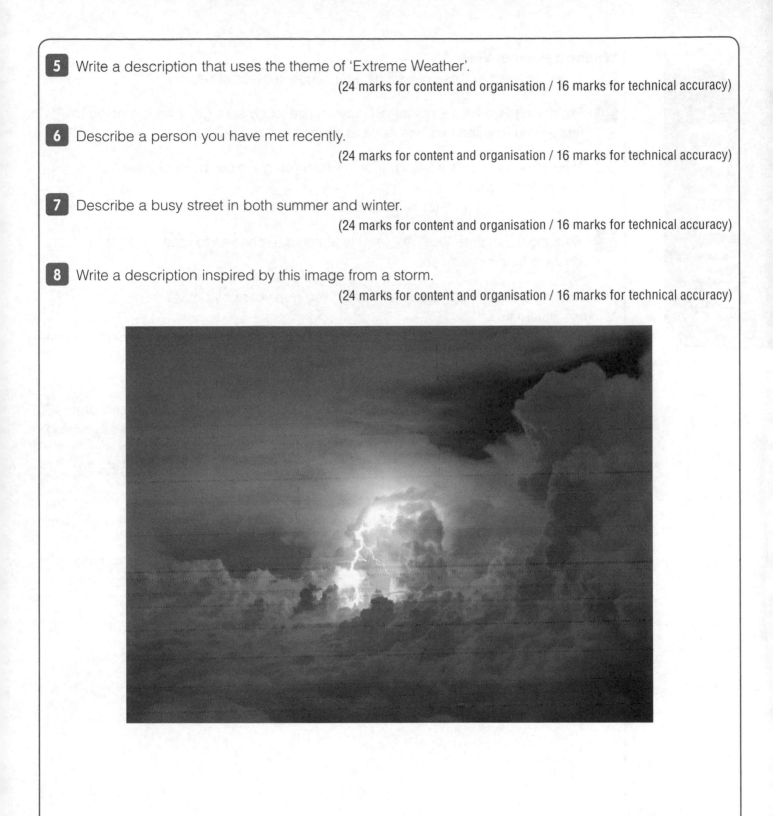

For more help on this topic, see Letts GCSE English Revision Guide pages 26–27.

Writing a Point of View

(Write your answers to these questions on a separate piece of paper.)

1 'People in this area are not taking recycling seriously enough. If we are going to improve our environment, we need to change our ways'

Write an article for your local paper in which you give your point of view on this statement.

(24 marks for content and organisation / 16 marks for technical accuracy)

2 'Reading transforms lives. We need to encourage children to read widely and regularly from an early age.'

Write an article for a magazine in which you give your point of view on this statement.

(24 marks for content and organisation / 16 marks for technical accuracy)

3 'Charity begins at home.'

Write an article for a website in which you give your point of view on this statement.

(24 marks for content and organisation / 16 marks for technical accuracy)

4 'Lack of exercise and over-eating are turning us into a nation of obese couch potatoes.'

Write an article for a broadsheet newspaper in which you give your point of view on this statement.

(24 marks for content and organisation / 16 marks for technical accuracy)

5 'Mobile phones should be banned in all schools.'

Write a letter to your head teacher in which you give your point of view on this statement.
(24 marks for content and organisation / 16 marks for technical accuracy)

6 'The proposals to build a new theme park in our town should be welcomed by us all. It will bring jobs, tourists and prosperity to our area.'

Write an article for your local paper in which you give your point of view on this statement.
(24 marks for content and organisation / 16 marks for technical accuracy)

7 'Reality television is a bad influence on children and adults alike. If the television companies do not voluntarily reduce the amount of reality TV they broadcast, the government will have to act.'

Write an article for a broadsheet newspaper in which you give your point of view on this statement.
(24 marks for content and organisation / 16 marks for technical accuracy)

8 'The only way to solve the health problems our young people are experiencing, is to ban fast food altogether'.

Write an article for your local paper in which you give your point of view on this statement.
(24 marks for content and organisation / 16 marks for technical accuracy)

For more help on this topic, see Letts GCSE English Revision Guide pages 30–33.

9 Write an article for a school or college magazine giving the arguments for and against school uniform.

(24 marks for content and organisation / 16 marks for technical accuracy)

10 The local council is proposing to reduce the speed limit in your town/city to 20 mph.

Write a letter to your local councillor in which you give your point of view on this proposal.

(24 marks for content and organisation / 16 marks for technical accuracy)

11 'Travel broadens the mind.'

Write an article for a magazine aimed at teenagers in which you give your point of view on this statement.

(24 marks for content and organisation / 16 marks for technical accuracy)

12 Examinations place too much pressure on young people. It is time to reduce the number of exams we take – if not abolish them altogether.'

Write an article for a broadsheet newspaper in which you give your point of view on this statement.

(24 marks for content and organisation / 16 marks for technical accuracy)

13 ''The minimum age for voting should be reduced from eighteen to sixteen.'

Write an article for a broadsheet newspaper paper in which you give your point of view on this statement.

(24 marks for content and organisation / 16 marks for technical accuracy)

14 'In our society old people are not given the respect that they deserve. It is up to the young to make sure that they are not only cared for but listened to and valued.'

Write an article for a magazine in which you give your point of view on this statement.

(24 marks for content and organisation / 16 marks for technical accuracy)

15 'Boys and girls learn more and achieve more if they are educated separately. '

Write an article for your local paper in which you give your point of view on this statement.

(24 marks for content and organisation / 16 marks for technical accuracy)

16 'Those who can, do. Those who can't, teach.'

Write an article for a website in which you give your point of view on this statement.

(24 marks for content and organisation / 16 marks for technical accuracy)

For more help on this topic, see Letts GCSE English Revision Guide pages 30–33.

Revising Anthology Poetry: Starter Questions

1 What is a simile? Choose an example from any poem in the anthology and explain what idea it conveys. (3 marks)

....

....

....

2 What is a metaphor? Choose an example from any poem in the anthology and explain what idea it conveys. (3 marks)

....

....

....

3 What is personification? Choose an example from any poem in the anthology and explain what idea it conveys. (3 marks)

....

....

....

4 What is alliteration? Choose an example from any poem in the anthology. Explain the effect of this technique on the poem. (3 marks)

....

....

....

5 What is onomatopoeia? Choose an example from any poem in the anthology. Explain the effect of this technique on the poem. (3 marks)

....

....

....

6 What is rhyme? Choose an example from any poem in the anthology. Explain the effect of this technique on the poem. (3 marks)

....

....

....

7 Find an example of each of the following structural devices from anywhere in the anthology and explain how your example is used to convey meaning in the poem.

(Write your answers to these questions on a separate piece of paper.)

    a) Repetition   (3 marks)

    b) Short Sentence   (3 marks)

    c) List   (3 marks)

    d) Enjambment   (3 marks)

    e) Pattern of three   (3 marks)

8 What is a persona? Choose an example from any poem in the anthology and explain who the persona is.   (3 marks)

9 What was the Romantic movement in poetry?

Pick a poem from the anthology written by a Romantic poet (Wordsworth, Shelley, Byron or Blake) and explain briefly how it reflects the ideas of the Romantic movement.   (6 marks)

For more help on this topic, see Letts GCSE English Revision Guide pages 44–45.

Love and Relationships

1 Compare the way the poets write about family relationships in 'Eden Rock' and one other poem from 'Love and Relationships'. (30 marks)

(Continue your answer on a separate piece of paper if you need to.)

2 Compare the way the poets write about unhappy relationships in 'The Farmer's Bride' and one other poem from 'Love and Relationships'. (30 marks)

(Continue your answer on a separate piece of paper if you need to.)

For more help on this topic, see Letts GCSE English Revision Guide pages 46–47.

Power and Conflict

1 Compare the way the poets write about war in 'The Charge of the Light Brigade' and one other poem from 'Power and Conflict'. (30 marks)

(Continue your answer on a separate piece of paper if you need to.)

2 Compare the way the poets write about power in 'Checking Out Me History' and one
other poem from 'Power and Conflict'.

(30 marks)

(Continue your answer on a separate piece of paper if you need to.)

Analysing Unseen Poetry

Answer both questions 1 and 2.

1 How does the poet present the shepherd's feelings for the woman he loves?
(Write your answer on a separate piece of paper.) (24 marks)

The Passionate Shepherd To His Love
by *Christopher Marlowe*

Come live with me and be my Love,

And we will all the pleasures prove

That hills and valleys, dale and field,

And all the craggy mountains yield.

There will we sit upon the rocks

And see the shepherds feed their flocks,

By shallow rivers, to whose falls

Melodious birds sing madrigals.

There will I make thee beds of roses

And a thousand fragrant posies,

A cap of flowers, and a kirtle

Embroider'd all with leaves of myrtle.

A gown made of the finest wool

Which from our pretty lambs we pull,

Fair linèd slippers for the cold,

With buckles of the purest gold.

A belt of straw and ivy buds

With coral clasps and amber studs:

And if these pleasures may thee move,

Come live with me and be my Love.

Thy silver dishes for thy meat

As precious as the gods do eat,

Shall on an ivory table be

Prepared each day for thee and me.

The shepherd swains shall dance and sing

For thy delight each May-morning:

If these delights thy mind may move,

Then live with me and be my Love.

2 In both 'The Passionate Shepherd to his Love' and 'Funeral Blues' the poets express their love. What are the similarities and/or differences between the ways the poets express their feelings? *(Write your answer on a separate piece of paper.)*

(8 marks)

Funeral Blues
by *W.H. Auden*

Stop all the clocks, cut off the telephone,

Prevent the dog from barking with a juicy bone,

Silence the pianos and with muffled drum

Bring out the coffin, let the mourners come.

Let aeroplanes circle moaning overhead

Scribbling on the sky the message He Is Dead,

Put crepe bows round the white necks of the public doves,

Let the traffic policemen wear black cotton gloves.

He was my North, my South, my East and West,

My working week and my Sunday rest,

My noon, my midnight, my talk, my song;

I thought that love would last for ever: I was wrong.

The stars are not wanted now: put out every one;

Pack up the moon and dismantle the sun;

Pour away the ocean and sweep up the wood.

For nothing now can ever come to any good.

For more help on this topic, see Letts GCSE English Revision Guide pages 48–53.

Answer both questions 3 and 4.

3 How does the poet present his experiences of World War One?   (24 marks)
(Write your answer on a separate piece of paper.)

Returning We Hear The Larks
by *Isaac Rosenberg*

Sombre the night is.

And though we have our lives, we know

What sinister threat lurks there.

Dragging these anguished limbs, we only know

This poison-blasted track opens on our camp –

On a little safe sleep.

But hark! joy – joy – strange joy.

Lo! heights of night ringing with unseen larks.

Music showering our upturned list'ning faces.

Death could drop from the dark

As easily as song –

But song only dropped,

Like a blind man's dreams on the sand

By dangerous tides,

Like a girl's dark hair for she dreams no ruin lies there,

Or her kisses where a serpent hides.

4 In both 'Returning to Hear the Larks' and 'Dirge for a Soldier', the poets present their experiences of war. What are the similarities and/or differences between the ways the poets convey their experiences? (8 marks)

(Write your answer on a separate piece of paper.)

Dirge For A Soldier
G.H. Boker

Close his eyes; his work is done!
What to him is friend or foeman,
Rise of moon, or set of sun,
Hand of man, or kiss of woman?

Lay him low, lay him low,
In the clover or the snow!
What cares he? He cannot know;
Lay him low!

As man may, he fought his fight,
Proved his truth by his endeavour;
Let him sleep in solemn night,
Sleep for ever and for ever.

Fold him in his country's stars,
Roll the drum and fire the volley!
What to him are all our wars,
What but death bemocking folly?

Leave him to God's watching eye;
Trust him to the hand that made him.
Mortal love weeps idly by;
God alone has power to aid him.

Lay him low, lay him low,
In the clover or the snow!
What cares he? He cannot know!
Lay him low!

For more help on this topic, see Letts GCSE English Revision Guide pages 48–53.

Answer both questions 5 and 6.

5 How does the poet present different childhood experiences?   (24 marks)
(Write your answer on a separate piece of paper.)

In Mrs Tilscher's Class
by *Carol Ann Duffy*

You could travel up the Blue Nile

with your finger, tracing the route

while Mrs Tilscher chanted the scenery.

'Tana. Ethiopia. Khartoum. Aswan.'

That for an hour,

then a skittle of milk

and the chalky Pyramids rubbed into dust.

A window opened with a long pole.

The laugh of a bell swung by a running child.

This was better than home. Enthralling books.

The classroom glowed like a sweetshop.

Sugar paper. Coloured shapes. Brady and Hindley

faded, like the faint, uneasy smudge of a mistake.

Mrs Tilscher loved you. Some mornings, you found

she'd left a gold star by your name.

The scent of a pencil slowly, carefully, shaved.

A xylophone's nonsense heard from another form.

Over the Easter term the inky tadpoles changed

from commas into exclamation marks. Three frogs

hopped in the playground, freed by a dunce

followed by a line of kids, jumping and croaking

away from the lunch queue. A rough boy

told you how you were born. You kicked him, but stared

at your parents, appalled, when you got back home.

That feverish July, the air tasted of electricity.

A tangible alarm made you always untidy, hot,

fractious under the heavy, sexy sky. You asked her

how you were born and Mrs Tilscher smiled

then turned away. Reports were handed out.

You ran through the gates, impatient to be grown

the sky split open into a thunderstorm.

6 In both 'In Mrs Tilscher's Class' and 'The Chimney Sweeper', the poets express feelings about childhood. What are the similarities and/or differences between the ways they express their feelings?

(8 marks)

(Write your answer on a separate piece of paper.)

The Chimney Sweeper
by *William Blake*

When my mother died I was very young,

And my father sold me while yet my tongue

Could scarcely cry 'weep weep weep weep!'

So your chimneys I sweep, and in soot I sleep.

There's little Tom Dacre, who cried when his head

That curled like a lamb's back, was shaved, so I said,

'Hush, Tom! Never mind it, for when your head's bare,

You know that the soot cannot spoil your white hair.'

And so he was quiet, and that very night,

As Tom was a-sleeping he had such a sight!

That thousands of sweepers, Dick, Joe, Ned, and Jack,

Were all of them locked up in coffins of black.

And by came an angel who had a bright key,

And he opened the coffins and set them all free;

Then down a green plain leaping, laughing they run

And wash in a river, and shine in the sun.

Then naked and white, all their bags left behind,

They rise upon clouds, and sport in the wind.

And the angel told Tom, if he'd be a good boy,

He'd have God for his father and never want joy.

And so Tom awoke, and we rose in the dark,

And got with our bags and our brushes to work;

Though the morning was cold, Tom was happy & warm –

So if all do their duty, they need not fear harm.

For more help on this topic, see Letts GCSE English Revision Guide pages 48–53.

Answer both questions 7 and 8.

7 How does the poet present his feelings about nature? (24 marks)
(Write your answer on a separate piece of paper.)

Daffodils
by *William Wordsworth*

I wander'd lonely as a cloud

That floats on high o'er vales and hills,

When all at once I saw a crowd,

A host of golden daffodils,

Beside the lake, beneath the trees

Fluttering and dancing in the breeze.

Continuous as the stars that shine

And twinkle on the milky way,

They stretch'd in never-ending line

Along the margin of a bay:

Ten thousand saw I at a glance

Tossing their heads in sprightly dance.

The waves beside them danced, but they

Out-did the sparkling waves in glee: -

A poet could not but be gay

In such a jocund company!

I gazed - and gazed - but little thought

What wealth the show to me had brought.

For oft, when on my couch I lie

In vacant or in pensive mood,

They flash upon that inward eye

Which is the bliss of solitude;

And then my heart with pleasure fills

And dances with the daffodils.

8 In both 'Daffodils' and 'Trees', the poets present their responses to nature. What are the similarities and/or differences between the ways in which they express their feelings? (8 marks)
(Write your answer on a separate piece of paper.)

Trees
by Philip Larkin

The trees are coming into leaf
Like something almost being said;
The recent buds relax and spread,
Their greenness is a kind of grief.

Is it that they are born again
And we grow old? No, they die too,
Their yearly trick of looking new
Is written down in rings of grain.

Yet still the unresting castles thresh
In full-grown thickness every May.
Last year is dead, they seem to say,
Begin afresh, afresh, afresh.

For more help on this topic, see Letts GCSE English Revision Guide pages 48–53.

Shakespeare

ROMEO AND JULIET (ACT 1 SCENE 1)
(Write your answer on a separate piece of paper.)

1 Starting with this extract, write about how Shakespeare presents the relationship between Romeo and Juliet.

Write about:
➤ how Shakespeare presents their relationship in this extract
➤ how Shakespeare presents their relationship in the play as a whole.

(30 marks)

At this point in the play, Romeo is explaining to Benvolio how Rosalind does not love him back.

BENVOLIO	What sadness lengthens Romeo's hours?
ROMEO	Not having that, which, having, makes them short.
BENVOLIO	In love?
ROMEO	Out –
BENVOLIO	Of love?
ROMEO	Out of her favour, where I am in love.
BENVOLIO	Alas, that love, so gentle in his view,
	Should be so tyrannous and rough in proof!
ROMEO	Alas, that love, whose view is muffled still,
	Should, without eyes, see pathways to his will!
	Where shall we dine? O me! What fray was here?
	Yet tell me not, for I have heard it all.
	Here's much to do with hate, but more with love.
	Why, then, O brawling love! O loving hate!
	O any thing, of nothing first create!
	O heavy lightness! serious vanity!
	Mis-shapen chaos of well-seeming forms!
	Feather of lead, bright smoke, cold fire, sick health!
	Still-waking sleep, that is not what it is!
	This love feel I, that feel no love in this.
	Dost thou not laugh?
BENVOLIO	No, coz, I rather weep.
ROMEO	Good heart, at what?
BENVOLIO	At thy good heart's oppression.
ROMEO	Why, such is love's transgression.
	Griefs of mine own lie heavy in my breast,
	Which thou wilt propagate, to have it prest
	With more of thine: this love that thou hast shown
	Doth add more grief to too much of mine own.
	Love is a smoke raised with the fume of sighs;
	Being purged, a fire sparkling in lovers' eyes;
	Being vex'd a sea nourish'd with lovers' tears:
	What is it else? a madness most discreet,
	A choking gall and a preserving sweet.
	Farewell, my coz

ROMEO AND JULIET (ACT 4 SCENE 5)

(Write your answer on a separate piece of paper.)

2 Starting with this extract, explain how Shakespeare presents Lord and Lady Capulet's feelings for Juliet.

Write about:
➤ how Shakespeare presents Lord and Lady Capulet's grief in this extract
➤ how Shakespeare presents Lord and Lady Capulet in the play as a whole.

(30 marks)

At this point in the play, on the morning of her wedding to Paris, Juliet has faked her death and is discovered by the Nurse and her parents.

LADY CAPULET	What noise is here?
NURSE	O lamentable day!
LADY CAPULET	What is the matter?
NURSE	Look, look! O heavy day!
LADY CAPULET	O me, O me! My child, my only life,
	Revive, look up, or I will die with thee!
	Help, help! Call help.
	*(Enter **Capulet**)*
CAPULET	For shame, bring Juliet forth; her lord is come.
NURSE	She's dead, deceased, she's dead; alack the day!
LADY CAPULET	Alack the day, she's dead, she's dead, she's dead!
CAPULET	Ha! let me see her: out, alas! she's cold:
	Her blood is settled, and her joints are stiff;
	Life and these lips have long been separated:
	Death lies on her like an untimely frost
	Upon the sweetest flower of all the field.
NURSE	O lamentable day!
LADY CAPULET	O woeful time!
CAPULET	Death, that hath ta'en her hence to make me wail,
	Ties up my tongue, and will not let me speak.
	*(Enter **Friar Laurence** and **Paris**, with Musicians)*
FRIAR LAURENCE	Come, is the bride ready to go to church?
CAPULET	Ready to go, but never to return.
	O son! the night before thy wedding-day
	Hath Death lain with thy wife. There she lies,
	Flower as she was, deflowered by him.
	Death is my son-in-law, Death is my heir;
	My daughter he hath wedded: I will die,
	And leave him all; life, living, all is Death's.

For more help on this topic, see Letts GCSE English Revision Guide pages 58–68.

Shakespeare

THE MERCHANT OF VENICE (ACT 1 SCENE 3)
(Write your answer on a separate piece of paper.)

3 Starting with this extract, write about how Shakespeare presents Shylock's feelings towards Christians.

Write about:
➤ how Shakespeare presents Shylock's feelings towards Antonio in this extract
➤ how Shakespeare presents Shylock's feelings about Christians in the play as a whole.

(30 marks)

At this point in the play, Shylock is considering Bassanio's request for a loan.

SHYLOCK	Three thousand ducats; I think I may take his bond.
BASSANIO	Be assured you may.
SHYLOCK	I will be assured I may; and, that I may be assured, I will bethink me. May I speak with Antonio?
BASSANIO	If it please you to dine with us.
SHYLOCK	Yes, to smell pork; to eat of the habitation which your prophet the Nazarite conjured the devil into. I will buy with you, sell with you, talk with you, walk with you, and so following, but I will not eat with you, drink with you, nor pray with you. What news on the Rialto? Who is he comes here?
	*(Enter **Antonio**)*
BASSANIO	This is Signior Antonio.
SHYLOCK (*Aside*)	How like a fawning publican he looks!
	I hate him for he is a Christian,
	But more for that in low simplicity
	He lends out money gratis and brings down
	The rate of usance here with us in Venice.
	If I can catch him once upon the hip,
	I will feed fat the ancient grudge I bear him.
	He hates our sacred nation, and he rails,
	Even there where merchants most do congregate,
	On me, my bargains and my well-won thrift,
	Which he calls interest. Cursed be my tribe,
	If I forgive him!
BASSANIO	Shylock, do you hear?
SHYLOCK	I am debating of my present store,
	And, by the near guess of my memory,
	I cannot instantly raise up the gross
	Of full three thousand ducats. What of that?
	Tubal, a wealthy Hebrew of my tribe,
	Will furnish me. But soft! how many months
	Do you desire? (*To **Antonio***) Rest you fair, good signior;
	Your worship was the last man in our mouths.

42 Shakespeare

THE MERCHANT OF VENICE (ACT 1 SCENE 2)

(Write your answer on a separate piece of paper.)

4 Starting with this extract, write about how Shakespeare presents the relationship between Portia and Nerissa.

Write about:
➤ how Shakespeare presents their relationship in this extract
➤ how Shakespeare presents their relationship in the play as a whole.

(30 marks)

At this point in the play, Portia is discussing her feelings about her current situation with Nerissa.

PORTIA	By my troth, Nerissa, my little body is aweary of this great world.
NERISSA	You would be, sweet madam, if your miseries were in the same abundance as your good fortunes are: and yet, for aught I see, they are as sick that surfeit with too much as they that starve with nothing. It is no mean happiness therefore, to be seated in the mean: superfluity comes sooner by white hairs, but competency lives longer.
PORTIA	Good sentences and well pronounced.
NERISSA	They would be better, if well followed.
PORTIA	If to do were as easy as to know what were good to do, chapels had been churches and poor men's cottages princes' palaces. It is a good divine that follows his own instructions: I can easier teach twenty what were good to be done, than be one of the twenty to follow mine own teaching. The brain may devise laws for the blood, but a hot temper leaps o'er a cold decree: such a hare is madness the youth, to skip o'er the meshes of good counsel the cripple. But this reasoning is not in the fashion to choose me a husband. O me, the word 'choose!' I may neither choose whom I would nor refuse whom I dislike; so is the will of a living daughter curbed by the will of a dead father. Is it not hard, Nerissa, that I cannot choose one nor refuse none?
NERISSA	Your father was ever virtuous; and holy men at their death have good inspirations: therefore the lottery, that he hath devised in these three chests of gold, silver and lead, whereof who chooses his meaning chooses you, will, no doubt, never be chosen by any rightly but one who shall rightly love. But what warmth is there in your affection towards any of these princely suitors that are already come?
PORTIA	I pray thee, over-name them; and as thou namest them, I will describe them; and, according to my description, level at my affection.

For more help on this topic, see Letts GCSE English Revision Guide pages 58–68.

MACBETH (ACT 3 SCENE 4)

(Write your answer on a separate piece of paper.)

5 Starting with this extract, explain how Shakespeare presents the changing character of Macbeth.

Write about:
➤ how Shakespeare presents Macbeth in this extract
➤ how Shakespeare presents Macbeth in the play as a whole.

(30 marks)

At this point in the play, Macbeth is recently crowned king and is holding a banquet. He has sent murderers to kill Banquo and Fleance.

MACBETH	You know your own degrees; sit down: at first
	And last the hearty welcome.
LORDS	Thanks to your majesty.
MACBETH	Ourself will mingle with society,
	And play the humble host.
	Our hostess keeps her state, but in best time
	We will require her welcome.
LADY MACBETH	Pronounce it for me, sir, to all our friends;
	For my heart speaks they are welcome.
	(First Murderer appears at the door)
MACBETH	See, they encounter thee with their hearts' thanks.
	Both sides are even: here I'll sit i' the midst:
	Be large in mirth; anon we'll drink a measure
	The table round.
	(Approaching the door)
	There's blood on thy face.
FIRST MURDERER	'Tis Banquo's then.
MACBETH	'Tis better thee without than he within.
	Is he dispatch'd?
FIRST MURDERER	My lord, his throat is cut; that I did for him.
MACBETH	Thou art the best o' the cut-throats: yet he's good
	That did the like for Fleance: if thou didst it,
	Thou art the nonpareil.
FIRST MURDERER	Most royal sir,
	Fleance is 'scaped.
MACBETH	Then comes my fit again: I had else been perfect,
	Whole as the marble, founded as the rock,
	As broad and general as the casing air:
	But now I am cabin'd, cribb'd, confined, bound in
	To saucy doubts and fears. But Banquo's safe?
FIRST MURDERER	Ay, my good lord: safe in a ditch he bides,
	With twenty trenched gashes on his head;
	The least a death to nature.

MACBETH (ACT 1 SCENE 7)

(Write your answer on a separate piece of paper.)

6 Starting with this extract, write about how Shakespeare presents the character of Lady Macbeth.
Write about:

➤ how Shakespeare presents Lady Macbeth in this extract

➤ how Shakespeare presents Lady Macbeth in the play as a whole.

(30 marks)

At this point in the play, King Duncan is at Dunsinane Castle. Despite initially agreeing to his wife's plan to kill the king, Macbeth has changed his mind.

MACBETH	We will proceed no further in this business:
	He hath honour'd me of late; and I have bought
	Golden opinions from all sorts of people,
	Which would be worn now in their newest gloss,
	Not cast aside so soon.
LADY MACBETH	Was the hope drunk
	Wherein you dress'd yourself? hath it slept since?
	And wakes it now, to look so green and pale
	At what it did so freely? From this time
	Such I account thy love. Art thou afeard
	To be the same in thine own act and valour
	As thou art in desire? Wouldst thou have that
	Which thou esteem'st the ornament of life,
	And live a coward in thine own esteem,
	Letting 'I dare not' wait upon 'I would,'
	Like the poor cat i' the adage?
MACBETH	Prithee, peace:
	I dare do all that may become a man;
	Who dares do more is none.
LADY MACBETH	What beast was't, then,
	That made you break this enterprise to me?
	When you durst do it, then you were a man;
	And, to be more than what you were, you would
	Be so much more the man. Nor time nor place
	Did then adhere, and yet you would make both:
	They have made themselves, and that their fitness now
	Does unmake you. I have given suck, and know
	How tender 'tis to love the babe that milks me:
	I would, while it was smiling in my face,
	Have pluck'd my nipple from his boneless gums,
	And dash'd the brains out, had I so sworn as you
	Have done to this.
MACBETH	If we should fail?
LADY MACBETH	We fail!
	But screw your courage to the sticking-place,
	And we'll not fail.

For more help on this topic, see Letts GCSE English Revision Guide pages 58–68.

Shakespeare

MUCH ADO ABOUT NOTHING (ACT 1 SCENE 1)
(Write your answer on a separate piece of paper.)

7 Starting with this extract, write about how Shakespeare presents the relationship between Benedick and Beatrice in *Much Ado About Nothing*.

Write about:
➤ how Shakespeare presents their relationship in this extract
➤ how Shakespeare presents their relationship in the play as a whole. (30 marks)

At this point in the play, Don Pedro and his men have arrived at Leonato's house and are being welcomed.

BENEDICK	If Signior Leonato be her father, she would not have his head on her shoulders for all Messina, as like him as she is.
BEATRICE	I wonder that you will still be talking, Signior Benedick: nobody marks you.
BENEDICK	What, my dear Lady Disdain! are you yet living?
BEATRICE	Is it possible disdain should die while she hath such meet food to feed it as Signior Benedick? Courtesy itself must convert to disdain, if you come in her presence.
BENEDICK	Then is courtesy a turncoat. But it is certain I am loved of all ladies, only you excepted: and I would I could find in my heart that I had not a hard heart; for, truly, I love none.
BEATRICE	A dear happiness to women: they would else have been troubled with a pernicious suitor. I thank God and my cold blood, I am of your humour for that: I had rather hear my dog bark at a crow than a man swear he loves me.
BENEDICK	God keep your ladyship still in that mind! so some gentleman or other shall 'scape a predestinate scratched face.
BEATRICE	Scratching could not make it worse, an 'twere such a face as yours were.
BENEDICK	Well, you are a rare parrot-teacher.
BEATRICE	A bird of my tongue is better than a beast of yours.
BENEDICK	I would my horse had the speed of your tongue, and so good a continuer. But keep your way, i' God's name; I have done.
BEATRICE	You always end with a jade's trick: I know you of old.

MUCH ADO ABOUT NOTHING (ACT 3 SCENE 2)

(Write your answer on a separate piece of paper.)

8 Starting with this extract, explain how Shakespeare presents the character of Don John in *Much Ado About Nothing*.

Write about:
➤ how Shakespeare presents Don John in this extract
➤ how Shakespeare presents Don John in the play as a whole.

(30 marks)

At this point in the play, it is the night before Claudio's wedding to Hero; Don John arrives with a plan to ruin the happy day.

DON JOHN	You may think I love you not: let that appear hereafter, and aim better at me by that I now will manifest. For my brother, I think he holds you well, and in dearness of heart hath holp to effect your ensuing marriage – surely suit ill spent and labour ill bestowed.
DON PEDRO	Why, what's the matter?
DON JOHN	I came hither to tell you; and, circumstances shortened, for she has been too long a talking of, the lady is disloyal.
CLAUDIO	Who, Hero?
DON PEDRO	Even she; Leonato's Hero, your Hero, every man's Hero:
CLAUDIO	Disloyal?
DON JOHN	The word is too good to paint out her wickedness; I could say she were worse: think you of a worse title, and I will fit her to it. Wonder not till further warrant: go but with me to-night, you shall see her chamber-window entered, even the night before her wedding-day: if you love her then, to-morrow wed her; but it would better fit your honour to change your mind.
CLAUDIO	May this be so?
DON PEDRO	I will not think it.
DON JOHN	If you dare not trust that you see, confess not that you know: if you will follow me, I will show you enough; and when you have seen more and heard more, proceed accordingly.
CLAUDIO	If I see any thing to-night why I should not marry her to-morrow in the congregation, where I should wed, there will I shame her.
DON PEDRO	And, as I wooed for thee to obtain her, I will join with thee to disgrace her.
DON JOHN	I will disparage her no farther till you are my witnesses: bear it coldly but till midnight, and let the issue show itself.
DON PEDRO	O day untowardly turned!
CLAUDIO	O mischief strangely thwarting!
DON JOHN	O plague right well prevented! so will you say when you have seen the sequel.

For more help on this topic, see Letts GCSE English Revision Guide pages 58–68.

Shakespeare

THE TEMPEST (ACT 5 SCENE 1)
(Write your answer on a separate piece of paper.)

9 Starting with this extract, write about how far Shakespeare presents Prospero's action as being driven by revenge.

Write about:
➤ how Shakespeare presents Prospero's motives in this extract
➤ how Shakespeare presents Prospero's motives in the play as a whole. **(30 marks)**

At this point in the play, Prospero traps Gonzalo, Alonso, Sebastian and Antonio in a magic circle before giving his judgement on each of them.

*(Re-enter **Ariel** before: then **Alonso**, with a frantic gesture, attended by **Gonzalo**; **Sebastian** and **Antonio** in like manner, attended by **Adrian** and **Francisco** they all enter the circle which **Prospero** had made, and there stand charmed; which **PROSPERO** observing, speaks:)*
A solemn air and the best comforter
To an unsettled fancy cure thy brains,
Now useless, boil'd within thy skull! There stand,
For you are spell-stopp'd.
Holy Gonzalo, honourable man,
Mine eyes, even sociable to the show of thine,
Fall fellowly drops. The charm dissolves apace,
And as the morning steals upon the night,
Melting the darkness, so their rising senses
Begin to chase the ignorant fumes that mantle
Their clearer reason. O good Gonzalo,
My true preserver, and a loyal sir
To him you follow'st! I will pay thy graces
Home both in word and deed. Most cruelly
Didst thou, Alonso, use me and my daughter:
Thy brother was a furtherer in the act.
Thou art pinch'd fort now, Sebastian. Flesh and blood,
You, brother mine, that entertain'd ambition,
Expell'd remorse and nature; who, with Sebastian,
Whose inward pinches therefore are most strong,
Would here have kill'd your king; I do forgive thee,
Unnatural though thou art. Their understanding
Begins to swell, and the approaching tide
Will shortly fill the reasonable shore
That now lies foul and muddy. Not one of them
That yet looks on me, or would know me Ariel,
Fetch me the hat and rapier in my cell:
I will discase me, and myself present
As I was sometime Milan: quickly, spirit;
Thou shalt ere long be free.

THE TEMPEST (ACT 1 SCENE 2)

(Write your answer on a separate piece of paper.)

10 Starting with this extract, write about how Shakespeare presents the relationship between Prospero and Ariel.

Write about:
➤ how Shakespeare presents their relationship in this extract
➤ how Shakespeare presents their relationship in the play as a whole.

(30 marks)

At this point in the play, Prospero has been checking that Ariel created the storm exactly as ordered.

PROSPERO	Ariel, thy charge Exactly is perform'd: but there's more work. What is the time o' the day?
ARIEL	Past the mid season.
PROSPERO	At least two glasses. The time 'twixt six and now Must by us both be spent most preciously.
ARIEL	Is there more toil? Since thou dost give me pains, Let me remember thee what thou hast promised, Which is not yet perform'd me.
PROSPERO	How now? moody? What is't thou canst demand?
ARIEL	My liberty.
PROSPERO	Before the time be out? no more!
ARIEL	I prithee, Remember I have done thee worthy service; Told thee no lies, made thee no mistakings, served Without or grudge or grumblings: thou didst promise To bate me a full year.
PROSPERO	Dost thou forget From what a torment I did free thee?
ARIEL	No.
PROSPERO	Thou dost, and think'st it much to tread the ooze Of the salt deep, To run upon the sharp wind of the north, To do me business in the veins o' the earth When it is baked with frost.
ARIEL	I do not, sir.
PROSPERO	Thou liest, malignant thing! Hast thou forgot The foul witch Sycorax, who with age and envy Was grown into a hoop? hast thou forgot her?
ARIEL	No, sir.
PROSPERO	Thou hast. Where was she born? speak; tell me.
ARIEL	Sir, in Argier.
PROSPERO	O, was she so? I must Once in a month recount what thou hast been, Which thou forget'st.

For more help on this topic, see Letts GCSE English Revision Guide pages 58–68.

JULIUS CAESAR (ACT 1 SCENE 2)

(Write your answer on a separate piece of paper.)

11 Starting with this extract, write about how Shakespeare presents the character of Julius Caesar.

Write about:
➤ how Shakespeare presents Julius Caesar in this extract
➤ how Shakespeare presents Julius Caesar in the play as a whole.

(30 marks)

At this point in the play, Julius Caesar is making his way through the streets to the Forum.

*(Flourish. Enter **Caesar**; **Antony**, for the course; **Calpurnia, Portia, Decius Brutus, Cicero, Brutus, Cassius,** and **Casca**; a great crowd following, among them a Soothsayer)*

CAESAR	Calpurnia!
CASCA	Peace, ho! Caesar speaks.
CAESAR	Calpurnia!
CALPURNIA	Here, my lord.
CAESAR	Stand you directly in Antonius' way,
	When he doth run his course. Antonius!
ANTONY	Caesar, my lord?
CAESAR	Forget not, in your speed, Antonius,
	To touch Calpurnia; for our elders say,
	The barren, touched in this holy chase,
	Shake off their sterile curse.
ANTONY	I shall remember:
	When Caesar says 'do this,' it is perform'd.
CAESAR	Set on; and leave no ceremony out.
	(Flourish)
SOOTHSAYER	Caesar!
CAESAR	Ha! who calls?
CASCA	Bid every noise be still: peace yet again!
CAESAR	Who is it in the press that calls on me?
	I hear a tongue, shriller than all the music,
	Cry 'Caesar!' Speak; Caesar is turn'd to hear.
SOOTHSAYER	Beware the ides of March.
CAESAR	What man is that?
BRUTUS	A soothsayer bids you beware the ides of March.
CAESAR	Set him before me; let me see his face.
CASSIUS	Fellow, come from the throng; look upon Caesar.
CAESAR	What say'st thou to me now? speak once again.
SOOTHSAYER	Beware the ides of March.
CAESAR	He is a dreamer; let us leave him: pass.

JULIUS CAESAR (ACT 3 SCENE 3)

(Write your answer on a separate piece of paper.)

12 Starting with this extract, explain how Shakespeare presents the character of Mark Antony in Julius Caesar.

Write about:
➤ how Shakespeare presents Antony in this extract
➤ how Shakespeare presents Antony in the play as a whole. **(30 marks)**

At this point in the play, the conspirators have come to the Forum to explain their reasons for assassinating Caesar. After Brutus's speech, Antony arrives with Caesar's body.

ANTONY   Friends, Romans, countrymen, lend me your ears;
I come to bury Caesar, not to praise him.
The evil that men do lives after them;
The good is oft interred with their bones;
So let it be with Caesar. The noble Brutus
Hath told you Caesar was ambitious:
If it were so, it was a grievous fault,
And grievously hath Caesar answer'd it.
Here, under leave of Brutus and the rest--
For Brutus is an honourable man;
So are they all, all honourable men--
Come I to speak in Caesar's funeral.
He was my friend, faithful and just to me:
But Brutus says he was ambitious;
And Brutus is an honourable man.
He hath brought many captives home to Rome
Whose ransoms did the general coffers fill:
Did this in Caesar seem ambitious?
When that the poor have cried, Caesar hath wept:
Ambition should be made of sterner stuff:
Yet Brutus says he was ambitious;
And Brutus is an honourable man.
You all did see that on the Lupercal
I thrice presented him a kingly crown,
Which he did thrice refuse: was this ambition?
Yet Brutus says he was ambitious;
And, sure, he is an honourable man.
I speak not to disprove what Brutus spoke,
But here I am to speak what I do know.
You all did love him once, not without cause:
What cause withholds you then, to mourn for him?
O judgment! thou art fled to brutish beasts,
And men have lost their reason. Bear with me;
My heart is in the coffin there with Caesar,
And I must pause till it come back to me.

For more help on this topic, see Letts GCSE English Revision Guide pages 58–68.

The 19th-Century Novel

The 19ᵗʰ Century Novel: Starter Questions

1 What sort of narrator does your novel have?

(2 marks)

2 Who is the protagonist of your novel?

(2 marks)

3 Briefly list five important characteristics of the protagonist.

(10 marks)

4 List five other important characters in your novel and explain the importance of each one.

(10 marks)

5 List five places that are important in your novel and explain the importance of each one.

(Write your answer on a separate piece of paper.)

(10 marks)

6 What do you consider to be the five most important incidents in your novel?

(Write your answer on a separate piece of paper.)

(10 marks)

Jane Eyre (Chapter 15)

(Write your answer on a separate piece of paper.)

1 Starting with the extract below, how far do you think that Brontë presents Jane as vulnerable and frightened?

Write about:
➤ how far she presents her as vulnerable and frightened in the extract
➤ how far she presents her as vulnerable and frightened in the novel as a whole.   (30 marks)

At this point in the novel, Jane is living and working at Thornfield.

I hardly know whether I had slept or not after this musing; at any rate, I started wide awake on hearing a vague murmur, peculiar and lugubrious, which sounded, I thought, just above me. I wished I had kept my candle burning: the night was drearily dark; my spirits were depressed. I rose and sat up in bed, listening. The sound was hushed.

I tried again to sleep; but my heart beat anxiously: my inward tranquillity was broken. The clock, far down in the hall, struck two. Just then it seemed my chamber-door was touched; as if fingers had swept the panels in groping a way along the dark gallery outside. I said, "Who is there?" Nothing answered. I was chilled with fear.

All at once I remembered that it might be Pilot, who, when the kitchen-door chanced to be left open, not unfrequently found his way up to the threshold of Mr. Rochester's chamber: I had seen him lying there myself in the mornings. The idea calmed me somewhat: I lay down. Silence composes the nerves; and as an unbroken hush now reigned again through the whole house, I began to feel the return of slumber. But it was not fated that I should sleep that night. A dream had scarcely approached my ear, when it fled affrighted, scared by a marrow-freezing incident enough.

This was a demoniac laugh—low, suppressed, and deep—uttered, as it seemed, at the very keyhole of my chamber door. The head of my bed was near the door, and I thought at first the goblin-laugher stood at my bedside—or rather, crouched by my pillow: but I rose, looked round, and could see nothing; while, as I still gazed, the unnatural sound was reiterated: and I knew it came from behind the panels. My first impulse was to rise and fasten the bolt; my next, again to cry out, "Who is there?"

Something gurgled and moaned. Ere long, steps retreated up the gallery towards the third-storey staircase: a door had lately been made to shut in that staircase; I heard it open and close, and all was still.

For more help on this topic, see Letts GCSE English Revision Guide pages 72–78.

Great Expectations (Chapter 29)
(Write your answer on a separate piece of paper.)

2 Starting with the extract below, how far do you think that Dickens presents Estella as unfeeling?

Write about:
➤ how far he presents her as unfeeling in the extract
➤ how far he presents her as unfeeling in the novel as a whole.

(30 marks)

At this point in the novel, Pip has travelled from London to see his family. He visits Miss Havisham and meets Estella, who he has not seen for a long time.

The air of completeness and superiority with which she walked at my side, and the air of youthfulness and submission with which I walked at hers, made a contrast that I strongly felt. It would have rankled in me more than it did, if I had not regarded myself as eliciting it by being so set apart for her and assigned to her.

The garden was too overgrown and rank for walking in with ease, and after we had made the round of it twice or thrice, we came out again into the brewery yard. I showed her to a nicety where I had seen her walking on the casks, that first old day, and she said, with a cold and careless look in that direction, "Did I?" I reminded her where she had come out of the house and given me my meat and drink, and she said, "I don't remember." "Not remember that you made me cry?" said I. "No," said she, and shook her head and looked about her. I verily believe that her not remembering and not minding in the least, made me cry again, inwardly,—and that is the sharpest crying of all.

"You must know," said Estella, condescending to me as a brilliant and beautiful woman might, "that I have no heart,—if that has anything to do with my memory."

I got through some jargon to the effect that I took the liberty of doubting that. That I knew better. That there could be no such beauty without it.

"Oh! I have a heart to be stabbed in or shot in, I have no doubt," said Estella, "and of course if it ceased to beat I should cease to be. But you know what I mean. I have no softness there, no—sympathy—sentiment—nonsense."

What was it that was borne in upon my mind when she stood still and looked attentively at me? Anything that I had seen in Miss Havisham? No. In some of her looks and gestures there was that tinge of resemblance to Miss Havisham which may often be noticed to have been acquired by children, from a grown person with whom they have been much associated and secluded, and which, when childhood is passed, will produce a remarkable occasional likeness of expression between faces that are otherwise quite different. And yet I could not trace this to Miss Havisham. I looked again, and though she was still looking at me, the suggestion was gone.

What was it?

"I am serious," said Estella, not so much with a frown (for her brow was smooth) as with a darkening of her face; "if we are to be thrown much together, you had better believe it at once. No!" imperiously stopping me as I opened my lips. "I have not bestowed my tenderness anywhere. I have never had any such thing."

The Strange Case of Dr Jekyll and Mr Hyde (Dr Jekyll's Full Statement Of The Case)
(Write your answer on a separate piece of paper.)

3 Starting with the extract below, write about how Stevenson presents Dr Jekyll's struggle with his Mr Hyde persona.

Write about:
➤ how he presents the struggle in the extract
➤ how he presents the struggle in the novel as a whole. (30 marks)

At this point in the novel, Dr Jekyll is explaining, in his statement, how the transformations into Mr Hyde became unwanted and difficult to control.

I was stepping leisurely across the court after breakfast, drinking the chill of the air with pleasure, when I was seized again with those indescribable sensations that heralded the change; and I had but the time to gain the shelter of my cabinet, before I was once again raging and freezing with the passions of Hyde. It took on this occasion a double dose to recall me to myself; and alas! Six hours after, as I sat looking sadly in the fire, the pangs returned, and the drug had to be re-administered.

In short, from that day forth it seemed only by a great effort as of gymnastics, and only under the immediate stimulation of the drug, that I was able to wear the countenance of Jekyll. At all hours of the day and night, I would be taken with the premonitory shudder; above all, if I slept, or even dozed for a moment in my chair, it was always as Hyde that I awakened. Under the strain of this continually-impending doom and by the sleeplessness to which I now condemned myself, ay, even beyond what I had thought possible to man, I became, in my own person, a creature eaten up and emptied by fever, languidly weak both in body and mind, and solely occupied by one thought: the horror of my other self. But when I slept, or when the virtue of the medicine wore off, I would leap almost without transition (for the pangs of transformation grew daily less marked) into the possession of a fancy brimming with images of terror, a soul boiling with causeless hatreds, and a body that seemed not strong enough to contain the raging energies of life. The powers of Hyde seemed to have grown with the sickliness of Jekyll. And certainly the hate that now divided them was equal on each side. With Jekyll, it was a thing of vital instinct. He had now seen the full deformity of that creature that shared with him some of the phenomena of consciousness, and was co-heir with him to death: and beyond these links of community, which in themselves made the most poignant part of his distress, he thought of Hyde, for all his energy of life, as of something not only hellish but inorganic. This was the shocking thing; that the slime of the pit seemed to utter cries and voices; that the amorphous dust gesticulated and sinned; that what was dead, and had no shape, should usurp the offices of life.

And this again, that that insurgent horror was knit to him closer than a wife, closer than an eye; lay caged in his flesh, where he heard it mutter and felt it struggle to be born; and at every hour of weakness, and in the confidence of slumber, prevailed against him and deposed him out of life.

For more help on this topic, see Letts GCSE English Revision Guide pages 72–78.

Pride and Prejudice (Chapter 3)

(Write your answer on a separate piece of paper.)

4 Starting with the extract below, how does Austen write about the theme of class and manners?

Write about:
➤ how she presents the theme of class and manners in the extract
➤ how she presents the theme of class and manners in the novel as a whole.

(30 marks)

At this point in the novel, the Bennett family meet Mr Bingley and his friend Mr Darcy at a ball.

Mr. Bingley was good-looking and gentlemanlike; he had a pleasant countenance, and easy, unaffected manners. His sisters were fine women, with an air of decided fashion. His brother-in-law, Mr. Hurst, merely looked the gentleman; but his friend Mr. Darcy soon drew the attention of the room by his fine, tall person, handsome features, noble mien, and the report which was in general circulation within five minutes after his entrance, of his having ten thousand a year. The gentlemen pronounced him to be a fine figure of a man, the ladies declared he was much handsomer than Mr. Bingley, and he was looked at with great admiration for about half the evening, till his manners gave a disgust which turned the tide of his popularity; for he was discovered to be proud; to be above his company, and above being pleased; and not all his large estate in Derbyshire could then save him from having a most forbidding, disagreeable countenance, and being unworthy to be compared with his friend.

Mr. Bingley had soon made himself acquainted with all the principal people in the room; he was lively and unreserved, danced every dance, was angry that the ball closed so early, and talked of giving one himself at Netherfield. Such amiable qualities must speak for themselves. What a contrast between him and his friend! Mr. Darcy danced only once with Mrs. Hurst and once with Miss Bingley, declined being introduced to any other lady, and spent the rest of the evening in walking about the room, speaking occasionally to one of his own party. His character was decided. He was the proudest, most disagreeable man in the world, and everybody hoped that he would never come there again. Amongst the most violent against him was Mrs. Bennet, whose dislike of his general behaviour was sharpened into particular resentment by his having slighted one of her daughters.

Elizabeth Bennet had been obliged, by the scarcity of gentlemen, to sit down for two dances; and during part of that time, Mr. Darcy had been standing near enough for her to hear a conversation between him and Mr. Bingley, who came from the dance for a few minutes, to press his friend to join it.

"Come, Darcy," said he, "I must have you dance. I hate to see you standing about by yourself in this stupid manner. You had much better dance."

"I certainly shall not. You know how I detest it, unless I am particularly acquainted with my partner. At such an assembly as this it would be insupportable. Your sisters are engaged, and there is not another woman in the room whom it would not be a punishment to me to stand up with."

"I would not be so fastidious as you are," cried Mr. Bingley, "for a kingdom! Upon my honour, I never met with so many pleasant girls in my life as I have this evening; and there are several of them you see uncommonly pretty."

"You are dancing with the only handsome girl in the room," said Mr. Darcy, looking at the eldest Miss Bennet.

"Oh! She is the most beautiful creature I ever beheld! But there is one of her sisters sitting down just behind you, who is very pretty, and I dare say very agreeable. Do let me ask my partner to introduce you."

"Which do you mean?" and turning round he looked for a moment at Elizabeth, till catching her eye, he withdrew his own and coldly said: "She is tolerable, but not handsome enough to tempt me; I am in no humour at present to give consequence to young ladies who are slighted by other men. You had better return to your partner and enjoy her smiles, for you are wasting your time with me."

A Christmas Carol (Stave One)

(Write your answer on a separate piece of paper.)

5 Starting with the extract below, explore how Dickens writes about poverty.

Write about:
➤ how he writes about poverty in the extract
➤ how he writes about poverty in the novel as a whole.

(30 marks)

At this point in the story, Scrooge receives two visitors in his counting-house.

"Scrooge and Marley's, I believe," said one of the gentlemen, referring to his list. "Have I the pleasure of addressing Mr. Scrooge, or Mr. Marley?"

"Mr. Marley has been dead these seven years," Scrooge replied. "He died seven years ago, this very night."

"We have no doubt his liberality is well represented by his surviving partner," said the gentleman, presenting his credentials.

It certainly was; for they had been two kindred spirits. At the ominous word "liberality," Scrooge frowned, and shook his head, and handed the credentials back.

"At this festive season of the year, Mr. Scrooge," said the gentleman, taking up a pen, "it is more than usually desirable that we should make some slight provision for the Poor and destitute, who suffer greatly at the present time. Many thousands are in want of common necessaries; hundreds of thousands are in want of common comforts, sir."

"Are there no prisons?" asked Scrooge.

"Plenty of prisons," said the gentleman, laying down the pen again.

"And the Union workhouses?" demanded Scrooge. "Are they still in operation?"

"They are. Still," returned the gentleman, "I wish I could say they were not."

"The Treadmill and the Poor Law are in full vigour, then?" said Scrooge.

"Both very busy, sir."

"Oh! I was afraid, from what you said at first, that something had occurred to stop them in their useful course," said Scrooge. "I'm very glad to hear it."

"Under the impression that they scarcely furnish Christian cheer of mind or body to the multitude," returned the gentleman, "a few of us are endeavouring to raise a fund to buy the Poor some meat and drink, and means of warmth. We choose this time, because it is a time, of all others, when Want is keenly felt, and Abundance rejoices. What shall I put you down for?"

"Nothing!" Scrooge replied.

"You wish to be anonymous?"

"I wish to be left alone," said Scrooge. "Since you ask me what I wish, gentlemen, that is my answer. I don't make merry myself at Christmas and I can't afford to make idle people merry. I help to support the establishments I have mentioned – they cost enough; and those who are badly off must go there."

"Many can't go there; and many would rather die."

"If they would rather die," said Scrooge, "they had better do it, and decrease the surplus population."

For more help on this topic, see Letts GCSE English Revision Guide pages 72–78.

***Frankenstein* (Chapter 16)**

(Write your answer on a separate piece of paper.)

6 Starting with the extract below, how does Shelley present the creature as unhappy and create sympathy for him?

Write about:
➤ how she presents him as unhappy and creates sympathy for him in the extract
➤ how she presents him as unhappy and creates sympathy for him in the novel as a whole.

(30 marks)

At this point in the novel, the Creature describes to Victor Frankenstein his feelings at being driven from the cottage by Felix.

"Cursed, cursed creator! Why did I live? Why, in that instant, did I not extinguish the spark of existence which you had so wantonly bestowed? I know not; despair had not yet taken possession of me; my feelings were those of rage and revenge. I could with pleasure have destroyed the cottage and its inhabitants and have glutted myself with their shrieks and misery.

"When night came I quitted my retreat and wandered in the wood; and now, no longer restrained by the fear of discovery, I gave vent to my anguish in fearful howlings. I was like a wild beast that had broken the toils, destroying the objects that obstructed me and ranging through the wood with a stag-like swiftness. Oh! What a miserable night I passed! The cold stars shone in mockery, and the bare trees waved their branches above me; now and then the sweet voice of a bird burst forth amidst the universal stillness. All, save I, were at rest or in enjoyment; I, like the arch-fiend, bore a hell within me, and finding myself unsympathized with, wished to tear up the trees, spread havoc and destruction around me, and then to have sat down and enjoyed the ruin.

"But this was a luxury of sensation that could not endure; I became fatigued with excess of bodily exertion and sank on the damp grass in the sick impotence of despair. There was none among the myriads of men that existed who would pity or assist me; and should I feel kindness towards my enemies? No; from that moment I declared everlasting war against the species, and more than all, against him who had formed me and sent me forth to this insupportable misery.

"The sun rose; I heard the voices of men and knew that it was impossible to return to my retreat during that day. Accordingly I hid myself in some thick underwood, determining to devote the ensuing hours to reflection on my situation.

"The pleasant sunshine and the pure air of day restored me to some degree of tranquillity; and when I considered what had passed at the cottage, I could not help believing that I had been too hasty in my conclusions. I had certainly acted imprudently. It was apparent that my conversation had interested the father in my behalf, and I was a fool in having exposed my person to the horror of his children. I ought to have familiarized the old De Lacey to me, and by degrees to have discovered myself to the rest of his family, when they should have been prepared for my approach. But I did not believe my errors to be irretrievable, and after much consideration I resolved to return to the cottage, seek the old man, and by my representations win him to my party.

The Sign of Four (Chapter 6)
(Write your answer on a separate piece of paper.)

7 Starting with this extract, write about how Conan Doyle presents the relationship between Holmes and Watson.

Write about:
➤ how he writes about their relationship in this extract
➤ how he writes about their relationship in the novel as a whole.

(30 marks)

Holmes and Watson have arrived at Pondicherry Lodge and have found the body of Bartholomew Sholto. They are now examining clues.

"Holmes," I said in a whisper, "a child has done this horrid thing."

He had recovered his self-possession in an instant.

"I was staggered for the moment," he said, "but the thing is quite natural. My memory failed me, or I should have been able to foretell it. There is nothing more to be learned here. Let us go down."

"What is your theory, then, as to those footmarks?" I asked eagerly when we had regained the lower room once more.

"My dear Watson, try a little analysis yourself," said he with a touch of impatience. "You know my methods. Apply them, and it will be instructive to compare results."

"I cannot conceive anything which will cover the facts," I answered.

"It will be clear enough to you soon," he said, in an offhand way. "I think that there is nothing else of importance here, but I will look."

He whipped out his lens and a tape measure and hurried about the room on his knees, measuring, comparing, examining, with his long thin nose only a few inches from the planks and his beady eyes gleaming and deep-set like those of a bird. So swift, silent, and furtive were his movements, like those of a trained bloodhound picking out a scent, that I could not but think what a terrible criminal he would have made had he turned his energy and sagacity against the law instead of exerting them in its defence. As he hunted about, he kept muttering to himself, and finally he broke out into a loud crow of delight.

"We are certainly in luck," said he. "We ought to have very little trouble now. Number One has had the misfortune to tread in the creosote. You can see the outline of the edge of his small foot here at the side of this evil-smelling mess. The carboy has been cracked, you see, and the stuff has leaked out."

"What then?" I asked.

"Why, we have got him, that's all," said he. "I know a dog that would follow that scent to the world's end. If a pack can track a trailed herring across a shire, how far can a specially trained hound follow so pungent a smell as this? It sounds like a sum in the rule of three. The answer should give us the - But hallo! here are the accredited representatives of the law."

For more help on this topic, see Letts GCSE English Revision Guide pages 72–78.

Drama: Revising Character

Remember to focus on how language, structure and form are used to convey meaning.
(All questions are worth 30 marks.)
(Write your answers on a separate piece of paper.)

A Taste of Honey

1. How does Delaney present Helen as a mother?

2. How does Delaney present Geoffrey as a social outcast?

An Inspector Calls

3. How does Priestley present Mrs Birling?

4. How does Priestley develop the character of Eric Birling?

Blood Brothers

5. How does Russell present Mrs Johnstone as a mother?

6. How does Russell present the character of Linda?

DNA

7. How does Kelly present the relationship between Phil and Lea?

8. How does Kelly show changes in the gang members?

History Boys

9. How does Bennett present the character of Scripps?

10. How does Bennett present the relationship between Hector and Dorothy?

Drama: Revising Themes

Remember to focus on how language, structure and form are used to convey meaning.
(All questions are worth 30 marks.)
(Write your answers on a separate piece of paper.)

A Taste of Honey

1 How does Delaney explore social taboos in the play?

2 How does Delaney use the character of Jo to explore the theme of hopes and fears?

An Inspector Calls

3 How does Priestley use the Inspector to explore the theme of judgement?

4 How does Priestley use Mr Birling to explore the theme of class?

Blood Brothers

5 How does Russell use different times to explore his ideas?

6 How does Russell explore the theme of brotherhood?

DNA

7 How does Kelly use the character of Adam to explore the theme of bullying?

8 How does Kelly explore the theme of leadership?

History Boys

9 How does Bennett use Dakin to explore the theme of attraction?

10 How does Bennett explore different ideas about education?

For more help on this topic, see Letts GCSE English Revision Guide pages 80–86.

Prose: Revising Character

Remember to focus on how language, structure and form are used to convey meaning. (All questions are worth 30 marks.)
(Write your answers on a separate piece of paper.)

The Lord of the Flies

1 How does Golding present the relationship between Ralph and Jack?

2 How does Golding present the relationship between Ralph and Piggy?

Animal Farm

3 How does Orwell present the differences between Snowball and Napoleon?

4 How does Orwell present the character of Benjamin?

Never Let Me Go

5 How does Ishiguro present the relationship between Kathy and Tommy?

6 How does Ishiguro present the character of Madame?

Anita and Me

7 How does Syal present the relationship between Meena and Anita?

8 How does Syal present the character of Sam?

Telling Tales

9 How do writers present female characters in 'The Odour of Chrysanthemums' and one other story from *Telling Tales*?

10 How do writers use first person narrators in 'Chemistry' and one other story from *Telling Tales*?

Pigeon English

11 How does Kelman present the relationship between Harri and Dean?

12 How does Kelman present the ways in which Harri changes?

Prose: Revising Themes

Remember to focus on how language, structure and form are used to convey meaning.
(All questions are worth 30 marks.)
(Write your answers on a separate piece of paper.)

The Lord Of The Flies

1 How does Golding explore the theme of law and order?

2 How does Golding use Ralph and Jack to explore the theme of leadership?

Animal Farm

3 How does Orwell use the pigs to explore the theme of corruption?

4 How does Orwell explore the theme of government?

Never Let Me Go

5 How does Ishiguro use Kathy, Ruth and Tommy to explore the theme of hopes and dreams?

6 How does Ishiguro explore the theme of not having freedom?

Anita and Me

7 How does Syal explore the theme of growing up?

8 How does Syal explore the clash between conformity and independence?

Telling Tales

9 How do writers explore ideas about identity in 'My Polish Teacher's Tie' and one other story from *Telling Tales*?

10 How do writers explore ideas about growing up in 'Chemistry' and one other story from *Telling Tales*?

Pigeon English

11 How does Kelman use Harri to explore the theme of right and wrong?

12 How does Kelman explore the theme of social problems?

For more help on this topic, see Letts GCSE English Revision Guide pages 80–86.

Practice Paper A GCSE ENGLISH LANGUAGE

Paper 1: Explorations in Creative Reading and Writing

Time allowed: 1 hour 45 minutes

There are 40 marks for **Section A** and 40 marks for **Section B**.

You are advised to spend about 15 minutes reading through the source and all five questions that you have to answer.

Section A: Reading
Answer **all** questions in this section.
You are advised to spend about 45 minutes on this section.
(Write your answers to the questions on a separate piece of paper.)

Source

This extract is the opening of a novel by Carol Shields. Published in 2002, it explores how the life of Reta Winters changes. She is a successful writer with a happy family and good friends until, one day, her eldest daughter suddenly drops out of university and stops speaking to anyone.

'Unless' by Carol Shields

IT HAPPENS THAT I am going through a period of great unhappiness and loss just now. All my life I've heard people speak of finding themselves in acute pain, bankrupt in spirit and body, but I've never understood what they meant. To lose. To have lost. I believed these visitations of darkness lasted only a few minutes or hours and that these saddened people, in between bouts, were occupied, as we all were, with the useful monotony of happiness. But happiness is not what I thought. Happiness is the lucky pane of glass you carry in your head. It takes all your cunning just to hang on to it, and once it's smashed you have to move into a different sort of life.

In my new life—the summer of the year 2000—I am attempting to "count my blessings." Everyone I know advises me to take up this repellent strategy, as though they really believe a dramatic loss can be replaced by the renewed appreciation of all one has been given. I have a husband, Tom, who loves me and is faithful to me and is very decent looking as well, tallish, thin, and losing his hair nicely. We live in a house with a paid-up mortgage, and our house is set in the prosperous rolling hills of Ontario, only an hour's drive north of Toronto. Two of our three daughters, Natalie, fifteen, and Christine, sixteen, live at home. They are intelligent and lively and attractive and loving, though they too have shared in the loss, as has Tom.

And I have my writing.

"You have your writing!" friends say. A murmuring chorus: But you have your writing, Reta. No one is crude enough to suggest that my sorrow will eventually become material for my writing, but probably they think it.

And it's true. There is a curious and faintly distasteful comfort, at the age of forty-three, forty-four in September, in contemplating what I have managed to write and publish during those impossibly childish and sunlit days before I understood the meaning of grief. "My Writing": this is a very small poultice to hold up against my damaged self, but better, I have been persuaded, than no comfort at all.

---

0 1 Read again the second paragraph of the source.

List **four** things from this part of the text that the narrator is grateful for. **[4 marks]**

0 2 Look in detail at the first paragraph of the source.

How does the writer use language and sentence structure here to describe different feelings?

You could include the writer's choice of:
- words and phrases
- language features and techniques
- sentence forms. **[8 marks]**

0 3 You now need to think about the **whole** of the source.

The text is from the opening of a novel. How has the writer structured the text to interest you as a reader?

You could write about:
- what the writer focuses your attention on in different paragraphs
- what information the writer holds back
- any other structural features that interest you. **[8 marks]**

0 4 Use the **whole** of the source to answer this question.

A student, having read this novel opening, said: 'The writer really brings the narrator to life. You can understand her; you feel like she's talking directly to you and confiding in you.'

To what extent do you agree?

In your response, you should:
- write about your own impression of the narrator
- evaluate how the writer has created these impressions
- support your opinions with quotations from the text. **[20 marks]**

You are advised to spend about 45 minutes on this section.

Write in full sentences.

You are reminded of the need to plan your answer.

You should leave enough time to check your work at the end.

(Write your answer on a separate piece of paper.)

| 0 | 5 |

You are going to enter a creative writing competition.

Either:

a) Write a description suggested by this picture:

Or:

b) Write the opening part of a story that conveys powerful emotions.

**(24 marks for content and organisation /
16 marks for technical accuracy.)
[40 marks]**

Practice Paper B GCSE ENGLISH LANGUAGE

Paper 2: Writers' Viewpoints and Perspectives

Time allowed: 1 hour 45 minutes

There are 40 marks for **Section A** and 40 marks for **Section B**.

You are advised to spend about 15 minutes reading through the source and all five questions that you have to answer.

Section A: Reading
Answer **all** questions in this section.
You are advised to spend about 45 minutes on this section.
(Write your answers to the questions on a separate piece of paper.)

Source A

This is an extract from 'Who On Earth Is Tom Baker?', the autobiography of the actor Tom Baker. Published in 1997, this extract describes his childhood during World War Two and his unusual ambition.

My first ambition was to be an orphan. During the war of 1939-45, Liverpool was a good place to be. All routine was broken by the fear of death from the Germans' bombs. The pleasure of being a child at that time is not easy to describe without seeming flippant. But it was drama, high drama: fires at night, the fires that burned people's houses down; bombs fell and left exotically shaped fragments in the form of shrapnel. And we collected it and traded it. As long as we were not hurt - and I wasn't - life seemed wonderful. At the gasworks one night a landmine, which was a bomb on a parachute, had descended gently and was hanging from one of the arms of the gasometer. Hundreds of people gathered and stood around, conjecturing about the size of the bomb. Bets were placed. The police and the fire brigade tried to get the people clear of the scene and, with difficulty, did so. Grumbling and arguing people were forced away from the danger area bitterly resenting the bossiness of the authorities.

Policemen and air-raid wardens and fire watchers loved the power they had to shout at their neighbours and tell them what to do, and they exercised it. In the shelters we sat all night or until the 'All Clear'. And people talked and talked and prayed and prayed that God would spare us. We were convinced, like all good Christians, that God was on our side.

The advantage of being an orphan sprang from the generosity of the American people. If your Dad or Mam was blown up then you really got some attention. Presents would arrive from America with a nice card from the President himself: funny hats and jackets that were considered very smart. At that time, the Superman comics were widely read and there were American soldiers all over the place. As American accents only reached us through the films, it was like being in a movie to meet them or to wear clothes that came from their country. We adored everything about America. We just could not get enough of it, from gum to caps to tee shirts with funny figures printed on them. We even copied the way the Americans walked, though Father Leonard, our parish priest, didn't like that bit of admiration. He disapproved of rolling buttocks.

The only drawback was that to qualify for the goodies your Mam had to be in Heaven. So I prayed hard that a bomb would drop on mine as she trudged home from the Sefton Arms.

It was common in those days for adults to ask quite small children what they wanted to be when they grew up. What a question in the middle of a world war! You can't ask that question now because it would be tactless as so many children are not going to become anything at all. But then everybody seemed to be asking children what their future would be. As if a child might know. These days when I see a child in Waitrose and smile and say, 'Hello, are you going to visit your Mum in her sheltered accommodation when you grow up?' it provokes glistening eyes and hollow laughter, And if you pursue it with, 'Or are you going to be a drugs dealer?' It may result in a snub. But in the days I'm talking about such enquiries were quite commonplace. Of course there was also a repertoire of stock answers from the child. One might answer: 'I'm going into the Merchant Navy, or the foreign missionaries, or the Adelphi Hotel, or Tate and Lyle's sugar factory' or, best of all, 'I'm going to stay at home with me Mam and look after her.' I don't know which precocious little sod first said that but the phrase passed into the language and made hard, sceptical men nod and bow their heads and strong, good-living women weep. It often led to a hug of such intensity that your nose would be broken. There were several broken-nosed five-year-olds in my school.

Source B

This is an extract from a letter by Admiral Sir Leopold George Heath KC, written during the Crimea War of 1853–56.

H.M.S. "Niger", May, 1854

May 13th. – One does not realise what war really is until one has either suffered oneself or seen its sad effects on one's friend. (...)

We saw the poor "Tiger" within thirty yards of the beach, over which rose cliffs a hundred and twenty feet high, crowned by no end of Russian field pieces and troops, the former shelling the "Tiger." We opened our fire as soon as we had got within range, but it was clear the "Tiger" was in the enemy's hands, for she had no colours up; she made no answer to my signal "How can I assist you?" and no return to the Russian guns, nor could we see anyone on board. The Russian fire was therefore probably intended to lure us to closer quarters, or perhaps to tempt our boats in to bring off the crew. However, Powell, the Commander of the "Vesuvius," came on board and said he thought he had seen the "Tiger's" crew marching up the hill side, and so as nothing more was to be done and there was no object in merely exchanging shots with the filed pieces, we steamed out of range and ceased firing. Smoke then began to rise from the "Tiger," and she was soon very soon in a blaze fore and aft; whether her own crew or the Russian shells had done it we don't know. In any case it was the best thing that could have happened, for with a garrison at Odessa of thirty thousand men and the ship thirty yards from the beach it would have been absurd to attempt and impossible to succeed in getting her off. I then hoisted a flag of truce and sent in a note to the Russian Commander asking for information about the crew. My boat was met half way by one from the shore, whose officer promised an answer should be sent, and explained (as well as a man speaking in Italian could to one who only understood English) that one officer (who turned out to be Captain Giffard) and one sailor were killed and three wounded, and that the rest were all prisoners, that the guns were all thrown overboard and the ship full of water. I waited for three hours, but no answer came. In the meantime the fire was doing its work, the masts fell in succession, and the whole of the upper works were in flames.

The poor "Tigers" seem to have done their best to get off, their boats were out and they had laid out a stern anchor and thrown their guns overboard; but it is difficult to account for their being all made prisoners, unless it was that they were so hard at work that they did not observe the rising of the fog in time to get away. Doubtless the first thing they saw was an overwhelming force almost over their heads; still I should have thought they would have taken to their boats and risked the chance of being shot in preference to the certainty of a prison.

The thick fog again came on at six, and I left to return to the Admiral. We had three men slightly wounded by shrapnel, but none of any consequence; several balls struck the ship's side, but only those coming through the ports could do much hard at that distance. Poor Mrs Giffard is at Malta with her children. The first lieutenant and surgeon are lately married, but one's sympathies are always more strong for those one knows than for strangers. It is altogether a most sad business, and I don't know when I have passed a more unhappy evening than I did last night. The only consolation is that although we have lost a ship the Russians have not gained one. I suppose they will in the course of time be able to dive for the engine, but it will be none the better for having been in salt water. I suppose experience will make us careful; the "Sidon" and "Niger" but narrowly escaped the "Tiger's" fate, they were neither of them so close to the shore, but both were well within range, and if guns had been brought down in any numbers they must probably have been abandoned. The fogs are wonderfully thick, but still we ought of course to be guided by the lead, and feel our way the more carefully.

0 1 Read again the last two paragraphs of Source A.

Choose **four** statements below that are **true**.

- Shade the boxes of the ones that you think are **true**.
- Choose a maximum of four statements.

A Tom Baker thinks it was strange, during a war, to ask children what they want to be when they grow up.

B Children never answered when they were asked what they wanted to be.

C People liked to hear a child say he would look after his mother.

D Tom Baker used to pray to be an orphan.

E The local pub was called the Red Lion.

F Tom Baker always talks politely to children when he meets them.

G Tate and Lyle's was the name of the local supermarket.

H Tom Baker's tone is quite jokey.

[4 marks]

0 2 You need to refer to **Source A** and **Source B** for this question.

Using details from **both** sources, write a summary of the writers' attitudes about death.   **[8 marks]**

0 3 You now need to refer **only** to **Source B**.

Looking at the second paragraph, how does Admiral Heath use language to convey his experience of war?   **[12 marks]**

0 4 For this question, you need to refer to the **whole of Source A** together with **Source B**.

Compare how the two writers convey their different attitudes to war.

In your answer you could:
- compare their different attitudes.
- compare the methods they use to convey their attitudes.
- support your ideas with quotations from both texts.   **[16 marks]**

Section B: Writing
You are advised to spend about 45 minutes on this section.
Write in full sentences.
You are reminded of the need to plan your answer.
You should leave enough time to check your work at the end.
(Continue your answer on a separate piece of paper.)

0 5   'Modern music is rubbish. It sounds awful, the lyrics are terrible, and the performers have no personality.'

Write an article for a broadsheet newspaper in which you explain your point of view about this statement.

(24 marks for content and organisation /
16 marks for technical accuracy.)
[40 marks]

Practice Paper C GCSE ENGLISH LITERATURE

Paper 1: Shakespeare and the 19th Century Novel

Time allowed: 1 hour and 45 minutes

- Answer **one** question from **Section A** and **one** question from **Section B**.
- The maximum mark for this paper is 64.
- AO4 will be assessed in **Section A**. There are 4 marks available for AO4 in **Section A** in addition to 30 marks for answering the question. AO4 assesses the following skills: Use a range of vocabulary and sentence structures for clarity, purpose and effect, with accurate spelling and punctuation.
- There are 30 marks for **Section B**.

Section A: Shakespeare
Answer the question from this section on your chosen text.
(Write your answer on a separate piece of paper.)

Macbeth

Read the following extract from Act 4 Scene 1 and then answer the question that follows.

At this point in the play, Macbeth has been presented with visions of the future by the witches. After they vanish, Lennox arrives.

LENNOX	Macduff is fled to England.
MACBETH	Fled to England!
LENNOX	Ay, my good lord.
MACBETH	Time, thou anticipatest my dread exploits:
	The flighty purpose never is o'ertook
	Unless the deed go with it; from this moment
	The very firstlings of my heart shall be
	The firstlings of my hand. And even now,
	To crown my thoughts with acts, be it thought and done:
	The castle of Macduff I will surprise;
	Seize upon Fife; give to the edge o' the sword
	His wife, his babes, and all unfortunate souls
	That trace him in his line. No boasting like a fool;
	This deed I'll do before this purpose cool.
	But no more sights!

0 1 Starting with this speech, explain how far you think Shakespeare presents Macbeth as an evil man.

Write about:
- how Shakespeare presents Macbeth in this speech
- how Shakespeare presents Macbeth in the play as a whole.

[30 marks]

AO4 [4 marks]

Romeo and Juliet

Read the following extract from Act 4 Scene 1 and answer the question that follows.

At this point in the play, Romeo has been exiled and Juliet has been told she must marry Paris. In desperation, she threatens to kill herself unless the Friar helps her.

JULIET	O shut the door! and when thou hast done so,
	Come weep with me; past hope, past cure, past help!
FRIAR LAURENCE	Ah, Juliet, I already know thy grief;
	It strains me past the compass of my wits:
	I hear thou must, and nothing may prorogue it,
	On Thursday next be married to this county.
JULIET	Tell me not, friar, that thou hear'st of this,
	Unless thou tell me how I may prevent it:
	If, in thy wisdom, thou canst give no help,
	Do thou but call my resolution wise,
	And with this knife I'll help it presently.
	God join'd my heart and Romeo's, thou our hands;
	And ere this hand, by thee to Romeo seal'd,
	Shall be the label to another deed,
	Or my true heart with treacherous revolt
	Turn to another, this shall slay them both:
	Therefore, out of thy long-experienced time,
	Give me some present counsel, or, behold,
	'Twixt my extremes and me this bloody knife
	Shall play the umpire, arbitrating that
	Which the commission of thy years and art
	Could to no issue of true honour bring.
	Be not so long to speak; I long to die,
	If what thou speak'st speak not of remedy.

0 2 Starting with this speech, explain how far you think Shakespeare presents Juliet as a strong-willed girl.

Write about:
• how Shakespeare presents Juliet in this speech
• how Shakespeare presents Juliet in the play as a whole.

[30 marks]

A04 [4 marks]

The Tempest

Read the following extract from Act 1 Scene 1 and answer the question that follows.

At this point in the play, Miranda has been upset by the sight of the shipwreck but Prospero reassures her that all is well.

PROSPERO	Be collected:
	No more amazement: tell your piteous heart
	There's no harm done.
MIRANDA	O, woe the day!
PROSPERO	No harm.
	I have done nothing but in care of thee,
	Of thee, my dear one, thee, my daughter, who
	Art ignorant of what thou art, nought knowing
	Of whence I am, nor that I am more better
	Than Prospero, master of a full poor cell,
	And thy no greater father.
MIRANDA	More to know
	Did never meddle with my thoughts.
PROSPERO	'Tis time
	I should inform thee farther. Lend thy hand,
	And pluck my magic garment from me. So:
	(Lays down his mantle)
	Lie there, my art. Wipe thou thine eyes; have comfort.
	The direful spectacle of the wreck, which touch'd
	The very virtue of compassion in thee,
	I have with such provision in mine art
	So safely ordered that there is no soul –
	No, not so much perdition as an hair
	Betide to any creature in the vessel
	Which thou heard'st cry, which thou saw'st sink. Sit down;
	For thou must now know farther.

0 3 Starting with this dialogue, explain how far you think Shakespeare presents Prospero as a loving father.

Write about:
- how Shakespeare presents Prospero in this dialogue
- how Shakespeare presents Prospero in the play as a whole.

[30 marks]
AO4 [4 marks]

The Merchant of Venice

Read the following extract from Act 1 Scene 3 and then answer the question that follows.

In this scene Antonio has just asked Shylock to lend him money.

SHYLOCK	Signor Antonio, many a time and oft
	In the Rialto have you rated me
	About my moneys and my usances.
	Still have I borne it with a patient shrug,
	For sufferance is the badge of all our tribe.
	You call me misbeliever, cut-throat dog,
	And spit upon my Jewish gaberdine,
	And all for use of that which is mine own.
	Well then, it now appears you need my help.
	Go to then. You come to me and you say,
	'Shylock, we would have moneys,' you say so,
	You, that did void thy rheum upon my beard
	And foot me as you spurn a stranger cur
	Over your threshold, moneys is your suit.
	What should I say to you? Should I not say,
	'Hath a dog money? Is it possible
	A cur can lend three thousand ducats?' Or
	Shall I bend low, and in a bondsman's key,
	With bated breath and whispering humbleness,
	Say this:
	'Fair sir, you spat on me on Wednesday last,
	You spurned me such a day, another time
	You called me dog, and for these courtesies
	I'll lend you thus much moneys?'

0 4 Starting with this speech, explain how far you think Shakespeare presents Shylock as a victim of anti-Semitism?

Write about:
- how Shakespeare presents Shylock in this speech
- how Shakespeare presents Shylock as a victim of anti-Semitism in the play as a whole.

[30 marks]

A04 [4 marks]

Much Ado about Nothing

Read the following extract from Act 5 Scene 4 and then answer the question that follows.

At this point Claudio has agreed to marry a woman he has never met in order to atone for his treatment of Hero.

CLAUDIO	Which is the lady I must seize upon?
ANTONIO	The same is she, and I do give you her.
CLAUDIO	Why, then she's mine. Sweet, let me see your face.
ANTONIO	No, that you shall not, till you take her hand
	Before this friar, and swear to marry her.
CLAUDIO	Give me your hand before this holy friar.
	I am your husband if you like of me.
HERO	And when she lived, I was your other wife,
	And when you loved, you were my other husband.
CLAUDIO	Another Hero!
HERO	Nothing certainer.
	One Hero died defiled, but I do live;
	And surely as I live I am a maid.
DON PEDRO	The former Hero, Hero that is dead.
LEONATO	She died, my lord, but whiles her slander lived.
FRIAR	All this amazement I can qualify,
	When, after the holy rites are ended,
	I'll tell you largely of fair Hero's death.
	Meantime let wonder seem familiar,
	And to the chapel let us presently

0 5 Starting with this extract, explain how Shakespeare presents the theme of honour.

Write about:
- how Shakespeare writes about honour in this extract
- how Shakespeare writes about honour in the play as a whole.

[30 marks]

AO4 [4 marks]

Julius Caesar

Read the following extract from Act 2 Scene 1 and then answer the question that follows.

Here, Brutus addresses his fellow conspirators before the murder of Caesar, after Cassius has argued that they should also kill Antony.

BRUTUS	Our course will seem too bloody, Caius Cassius,
	To cut the head off and then hack the limbs,
	Like wrath in death and envy afterwards –
	For Antony is but a limb of Caesar.
	Let's be sacrificers, but not butchers, Caius.
	We all stand up against the spirit of Caesar,
	And in the spirit of men there is no blood.
	O, that we could come by Caesar's spirit,
	And not dismember Caesar! But, alas,
	Caesar must bleed for it. And, gentle friends,
	Let's kill him boldly, but not wrathfully.
	Let's carve him as a dish fit for the gods,
	Not hew him as a carcass fit for hounds.
	And let our hearts, as subtle masters do,
	Stir up their servants to an act of rage,
	And after seem to chide 'em. This shall make
	Our purpose necessary, and not envious;
	Which so appearing to the common eyes,
	We shall be called purgers, not murderers.
	And for Mark Antony, think not of him,
	For he can do no more than Caesar's arm
	When Caesar's head is off.

0 6 Starting with this speech, explain how far you think that Shakespeare presents Brutus as an honourable man.

Write about:
- how Shakespeare presents Brutus in this speech
- how Shakespeare presents Brutus in the play as a whole.

[30 marks]

AO4 [4 marks]

Section B: The 19th Century Novel
Answer the question from this section on your chosen text.
(Write your answer on a separate piece of paper.)

Charles Dickens: *Great Expectations*

Read the following extract from Chapter 2 and then answer the question that follows.

In this extract, Dickens introduces the characters of Joe and Mrs Joe.

> Joe was a fair man, with curls of flaxen hair on each side of his smooth face, and with eyes of such a very undecided blue that they seemed to have somehow got mixed with their own whites. He was a mild, good-natured, sweet-tempered, easy-going, foolish, dear fellow,—a sort of Hercules in strength, and also in weakness.
>
> My sister, Mrs. Joe, with black hair and eyes, had such a prevailing redness of skin that I sometimes used to wonder whether it was possible she washed herself with a nutmeg-grater instead of soap. She was tall and bony, and almost always wore a coarse apron, fastened over her figure behind with two loops, and having a square impregnable bib in front, that was stuck full of pins and needles. She made it a powerful merit in herself, and a strong reproach against Joe, that she wore this apron so much. Though I really see no reason why she should have worn it at all; or why, if she did wear it at all, she should not have taken it off, every day of her life.
>
> Joe's forge adjoined our house, which was a wooden house, as many of the dwellings in our country were,—most of them, at that time. When I ran home from the churchyard, the forge was shut up, and Joe was sitting alone in the kitchen. Joe and I being fellow-sufferers, and having confidences as such, Joe imparted a confidence to me, the moment I raised the latch of the door and peeped in at him opposite to it, sitting in the chimney corner.
>
> "Mrs. Joe has been out a dozen times, looking for you, Pip. And she's out now, making it a baker's dozen."
>
> "Is she?"
>
> "Yes, Pip," said Joe; "and what's worse, she's got Tickler with her."
>
> At this dismal intelligence, I twisted the only button on my waistcoat round and round, and looked in great depression at the fire. Tickler was a wax-ended piece of cane, worn smooth by collision with my tickled frame.
>
> "She sot down," said Joe, "and she got up, and she made a grab at Tickler, and she rampaged out. That's what she did," said Joe, slowly clearing the fire between the lower bars with the poker, and looking at it; "she Ram-paged out, Pip."
>
> "Has she been gone long, Joe?" I always treated him as a larger species of child, and as no more than my equal.
>
> "Well," said Joe, glancing up at the Dutch clock, "she's been on the rampage, this last spell, about five minutes, Pip. She's a coming! Get behind the door, old chap, and have the jack-towel betwixt you."

| 0 | 7 | Starting with this extract, how does Dickens present Joe as a kind but weak character?

Write about:
- how Dickens presents Joe in this extract
- how Dickens presents Joe as a kind but weak man in the novel as a whole.   **[30 marks]**

Charlotte Brontë: *Jane Eyre*

Read the following extract from Chapter 7 and then answer the question that follows.

In this extract, Jane is a student at Lowood School. Mr Brocklehurst has arrived and ordered that Jane be made to stand on a stool in front of everyone.

"Ladies," said he, turning to his family, "Miss Temple, teachers, and children, you all see this girl?"

Of course they did; for I felt their eyes directed like burning-glasses against my scorched skin.

"You see she is yet young; you observe she possesses the ordinary form of childhood; God has graciously given her the shape that He has given to all of us; no signal deformity points her out as a marked character. Who would think that the Evil One had already found a servant and agent in her? Yet such, I grieve to say, is the case."

A pause—in which I began to steady the palsy of my nerves, and to feel that the Rubicon was passed; and that the trial, no longer to be shirked, must be firmly sustained.

"My dear children," pursued the black marble clergyman, with pathos, "this is a sad, a melancholy occasion; for it becomes my duty to warn you, that this girl, who might be one of God's own lambs, is a little castaway: not a member of the true flock, but evidently an interloper and an alien. You must be on your guard against her; you must shun her example; if necessary, avoid her company, exclude her from your sports, and shut her out from your converse. Teachers, you must watch her: keep your eyes on her movements, weigh well her words, scrutinise her actions, punish her body to save her soul: if, indeed, such salvation be possible, for (my tongue falters while I tell it) this girl, this child, the native of a Christian land, worse than many a little heathen who says its prayers to Brahma and kneels before Juggernaut—this girl is—a liar!"

Now came a pause of ten minutes, during which I, by this time in perfect possession of my wits, observed all the female Brocklehursts produce their pocket-handkerchiefs and apply them to their optics, while the elderly lady swayed herself to and fro, and the two younger ones whispered, "How shocking!" Mr. Brocklehurst resumed.

"This I learned from her benefactress; from the pious and charitable lady who adopted her in her orphan state, reared her as her own daughter, and whose kindness, whose generosity the unhappy girl repaid by an ingratitude so bad, so dreadful, that at last her excellent patroness was obliged to separate her from her own young ones, fearful lest her vicious example should contaminate their purity: she has sent her here to be healed, even as the Jews of old sent their diseased to the troubled pool of Bethesda; and, teachers, superintendent, I beg of you not to allow the waters to stagnate round her."

With this sublime conclusion, Mr. Brocklehurst adjusted the top button of his surtout, muttered something to his family, who rose, bowed to Miss Temple, and then all the great people sailed in state from the room. Turning at the door, my judge said—

"Let her stand half-an-hour longer on that stool, and let no one speak to her during the remainder of the day."

0 8 Starting with this extract, how does Brontë make us feel sympathy for Jane?

Write about:
- how Brontë presents Jane in this extract
- how Brontë makes us feel sympathy for Jane in the novel as a whole.

[30 marks]

Mary Shelley: *Frankenstein*

Read the following extract from Chapter 5 and then answer the question that follows.

In this extract, Victor Frankenstein has succeeded in bringing the Creature to life.

It was on a dreary night of November that I beheld the accomplishment of my toils. With an anxiety that almost amounted to agony, I collected the instruments of life around me, that I might infuse a spark of being into the lifeless thing that lay at my feet. It was already one in the morning; the rain pattered dismally against the panes, and my candle was nearly burnt out, when, by the glimmer of the half-extinguished light, I saw the dull yellow eye of the creature open; it breathed hard, and a convulsive motion agitated its limbs.

How can I describe my emotions at this catastrophe, or how delineate the wretch whom with such infinite pains and care I had endeavoured to form? His limbs were in proportion, and I had selected his features as beautiful. Beautiful! Great God! His yellow skin scarcely covered the work of muscles and arteries beneath; his hair was of a lustrous black, and flowing; his teeth of a pearly whiteness; but these luxuriances only formed a more horrid contrast with his watery eyes, that seemed almost of the same colour as the dun-white sockets in which they were set, his shrivelled complexion and straight black lips.

The different accidents of life are not so changeable as the feelings of human nature. I had worked hard for nearly two years, for the sole purpose of infusing life into an inanimate body. For this I had deprived myself of rest and health. I had desired it with an ardour that far exceeded moderation; but now that I had finished, the beauty of the dream vanished, and breathless horror and disgust filled my heart. Unable to endure the aspect of the being I had created, I rushed out of the room and continued a long time traversing my bed-chamber, unable to compose my mind to sleep. At length lassitude succeeded to the tumult I had before endured, and I threw myself on the bed in my clothes, endeavouring to seek a few moments of forgetfulness. But it was in vain; I slept, indeed, but I was disturbed by the wildest dreams. I thought I saw Elizabeth, in the bloom of health, walking in the streets of Ingolstadt. Delighted and surprised, I embraced her, but as I imprinted the first kiss on her lips, they became livid with the hue of death; her features appeared to change, and I thought that I held the corpse of my dead mother in my arms; a shroud enveloped her form, and I saw the grave-worms crawling in the folds of the flannel. I started from my sleep with horror; a cold dew covered my forehead, my teeth chattered, and every limb became convulsed; when, by the dim and yellow light of the moon, as it forced its way through the window shutters, I beheld the wretch—the miserable monster whom I had created. He held up the curtain of the bed; and his eyes, if eyes they may be called, were fixed on me. His jaws opened, and he muttered some inarticulate sounds, while a grin wrinkled his cheeks. He might have spoken, but I did not hear; one hand was stretched out, seemingly to detain me, but I escaped and rushed downstairs. I took refuge in the courtyard belonging to the house which I inhabited, where I remained during the rest of the night, walking up and down in the greatest agitation, listening attentively, catching and fearing each sound as if it were to announce the approach of the demoniacal corpse to which I had so miserably given life.

0 9 Starting with this extract, how does Shelley present Victor Frankenstein's dislike of his creation?

Write about:
- how Shelley presents Victor's reactions to the Creature in this extract.
- how Shelley presents Victor's dislike of the Creature in the novel as a whole. **[30 marks]**

Jane Austen: *Pride and Prejudice*

Read the following extract from Chapter 4 and then answer the question that follows.

In this extract, Jane and Elizabeth are discussing Mr Bingley.

When Jane and Elizabeth were alone, the former, who had been cautious in her praise of Mr. Bingley before, expressed to her sister how very much she admired him.

"He is just what a young man ought to be," said she, "sensible, good-humoured, lively; and I never saw such happy manners! -- so much ease, with such perfect good-breeding!"

"He is also handsome," said Elizabeth; "which a young man ought likewise to be, if he possibly can. His character is thereby complete."

"I was very much flattered by his asking me to dance a second time. I did not expect such a compliment."

"Did not you? I did for you. But that is one great difference between us. Compliments always take you by surprise, and me never. What could be more natural than his asking you again? He could not help seeing that you were about five times as pretty as every other woman in the room. No thanks to his gallantry for that. Well, he certainly is very agreeable, and I give you leave to like him. You have liked many a stupider person."

"Dear Lizzy!"

"Oh! you are a great deal too apt, you know, to like people in general. You never see a fault in anybody. All the world are good and agreeable in your eyes. I never heard you speak ill of a human being in my life."

"I would wish not to be hasty in censuring any one; but I always speak what I think."

"I know you do; and it is that which makes the wonder. With your good sense to be so honestly blind to the follies and nonsense of others! Affectation of candour is common enough; -- one meets it everywhere. But to be candid without ostentation or design -- to take the good of everybody's character and make it still better, and say nothing of the bad -- belongs to you alone. And so you like this man's sisters too, do you? Their manners are not equal to his."

---

1 0 Starting with this extract, explore how Austen presents the characters of Jane and Mr Bingley.

Write about:
- how she presents them in this extract
- how she presents them in the novel as a whole.

[30 marks]

Charles Dickens: *A Christmas Carol*

Read the following extract from Stave (Chapter) 2 and then answer the question that follows.

In this extract, Scrooge meets the Ghost of Christmas Past.

It was a strange figure -- like a child: yet not so like a child as like an old man, viewed through some supernatural medium, which gave him the appearance of having receded from the view, and being diminished to a child's proportions. Its hair, which hung about its neck and down its back, was white as if with age; and yet the face had not a wrinkle in it, and the tenderest bloom was on the skin. The arms were very long and muscular; the hands the same, as if its hold were of uncommon strength. Its legs and feet, most delicately formed, were, like those upper members, bare. It wore a tunic of the purest white and round its waist was bound a lustrous belt, the sheen of which was beautiful. It held a branch of fresh green holly in its hand; and, in singular contradiction of that wintry emblem, had its dress trimmed with summer flowers. But the strangest thing about it was, that from the crown of its head there sprung a bright clear jet of light, by which all this was visible; and which was doubtless the occasion of its using, in its duller moments, a great extinguisher for a cap, which it now held under its arm.

Even this, though, when Scrooge looked at it with increasing steadiness, was not its strangest quality. For as its belt sparkled and glittered now in one part and now in another, and what was light one instant, at another time was dark, so the figure itself fluctuated in its distinctness: being now a thing with one arm, now with one leg, now with twenty legs, now a pair of legs without a head, now a head without a body: of which dissolving parts, no outline would be visible in the dense gloom wherein they melted away. And in the very wonder of this, it would be itself again; distinct and clear as ever.

``Are you the Spirit, sir, whose coming was foretold to me?'' asked Scrooge.

``I am!''

The voice was soft and gentle. Singularly low, as if instead of being so close beside him, it were at a distance.

``Who, and what are you?'' Scrooge demanded.

``I am the Ghost of Christmas Past.''

``Long past?'' inquired Scrooge: observant of its dwarfish stature.

``No. Your past.''

1 1 Starting with this extract, explain the significance of the three spirits of Christmas and their effect on Scrooge.
Write about:
- how Dickens presents the Ghost of Christmas Past in this extract
- how Dickens presents the Ghosts of Christmas Past, Christmas Present and Christmas yet to Come in the novel as a whole.

[30 marks]

Robert Louis Stevenson: *The Strange Case of Dr Jekyll and Mr Hyde*

Read the following extract from 'Dr Lanyon's Narrative' and then answer the question that follows.

In this extract, Dr Lanyon watches as Hyde changes back into Jekyll.

"And now," said he, "to settle what remains. Will you be wise? will you be guided? will you suffer me to take this glass in my hand and to go forth from your house without further parley? or has the greed of curiosity too much command of you? Think before you answer, for it shall be done as you decide. As you decide, you shall be left as you were before, and neither richer nor wiser, unless the sense of service rendered to a man in mortal distress may be counted as a kind of riches of the soul. Or, if you shall so prefer to choose, a new province of knowledge and new avenues to fame and power shall be laid open to you, here, in this room, upon the instant; and your sight shall be blasted by a prodigy to stagger the unbelief of Satan."

"Sir," said I, affecting a coolness that I was far from truly possessing, "you speak enigmas, and you will perhaps not wonder that I hear you with no very strong impression of belief. But I have gone too far in the way of inexplicable services to pause before I see the end."

"It is well," replied my visitor. "Lanyon, you remember your vows: what follows is under the seal of our profession. And now, you who have so long been bound to the most narrow and material views, you who have denied the virtue of transcendental medicine, you who have derided your superiors--behold!"

He put the glass to his lips and drank at one gulp. A cry followed; he reeled, staggered, clutched at the table and held on, staring with injected eyes, gasping with open mouth; and as I looked there came, I thought, a change--he seemed to swell-- his face became suddenly black and the features seemed to melt and alter--and the next moment, I had sprung to my feet and leaped back against the wall, my arms raised to shield me from that prodigy, my mind submerged in terror.

"O God!" I screamed, and "O God!" again and again; for there before my eyes--pale and shaken, and half fainting, and groping before him with his hands, like a man restored from death--there stood Henry Jekyll!

What he told me in the next hour, I cannot bring my mind to set on paper. I saw what I saw, I heard what I heard, and my soul sickened at it; and yet now when that sight has faded from my eyes, I ask myself if I believe it, and I cannot answer. My life is shaken to its roots; sleep has left me; the deadliest terror sits by me at all hours of the day and night; and I feel that my days are numbered, and that I must die; and yet I shall die incredulous. As for the moral turpitude that man unveiled to me, even with tears of penitence, I can not, even in memory, dwell on it without a start of horror. I will say but one thing, Utterson, and that (if you can bring your mind to credit it) will be more than enough. The creature who crept into my house that night was, on Jekyll's own confession, known by the name of Hyde and hunted for in every corner of the land as the murderer of Carew.

---

1 2 Starting with this extract, how does Stevenson use Jekyll and Hyde to explore ideas about good and evil?

Write about:
- how Stevenson presents ideas about good and evil in this extract
- how Stevenson presents ideas about good and evil in the novel as a whole

[30 marks]

Sir Arthur Conan Doyle: *The Sign of Four*

Read the following extract from Chapter 11 and then answer the question that follows.

In this extract, Dr Watson has brought a box, supposed to contain the treasure, to Miss Morstan.

She glanced at the iron box.

"What a pretty box!" she said, stooping over it. "This is Indian work, I suppose?"

"Yes; it is Benares metal-work."

"And so heavy!" she exclaimed, trying to raise it. "The box alone must be of some value. Where is the key?"

"Small threw it into the Thames," I answered. "I must borrow Mrs. Forrester's poker."

There was in the front a thick and broad hasp, wrought in the image of a sitting Buddha. Under this I thrust the end of the poker and twisted it outward as a lever. The hasp sprang open with a loud snap. With trembling fingers I flung back the lid. We both stood gazing in astonishment. The box was empty!

No wonder that it was heavy. The ironwork was two-thirds of an inch thick all round. It was massive, well made, and solid, like a chest constructed to carry things of great price, but not one shred or crumb of metal or jewellery lay within it. It was absolutely and completely empty.

"The treasure is lost," said Miss Morstan calmly.

As I listened to the words and realized what they meant, a great shadow seemed to pass from my soul. I did not know how this Agra treasure had weighed me down until now that it was finally removed. It was selfish, no doubt, disloyal, wrong, but I could realize nothing save that the golden barrier was gone from between us.

---

1 3 Starting with this extract, explore how Conan Doyle presents the themes of wealth and greed.

Write about:
- how Conan Doyle writes about wealth and greed in this extract
- how Conan Doyle writes about wealth and greed in the novel as a whole.

[30 marks]

Practice Paper D GCSE ENGLISH LITERATURE

Paper 2: Modern Texts and Poetry

Time allowed: 2 hours 15 minutes

- Answer **one** question from **Section A**, **one** question from **Section B** and **both** questions in **Section C**.
- The maximum mark for this paper is 96.
- AO4 will be assessed in **Section A**. There are 4 marks available for AO4 in **Section A** in addition to 30 marks for answering the question. AO4 assesses the following skills: Use a range of vocabulary and sentence structures for clarity, purpose and effect, with accurate spelling and punctuation.
- There are 30 marks for **Section B** and 32 marks for **Section C**.

Section A: Modern Prose or Drama
Answer **one** question from this section on your chosen text.
(Write your answer on a separate piece of paper.)

JB Priestley: *An Inspector Calls*

`0` `1` How does Priestley present the relationship between the Inspector and Mr Birling?
Write about:
- how the Inspector behaves towards Mr Birling
- how Mr Birling responds to the Inspector.   **[30 marks] AO4 [4 marks]**

`0` `2` How does Priestley use Sheila to present the theme of guilt?
Write about:
- where Sheila does and doesn't show guilt
- how Priestley presents his ideas in the way that he writes.   **[30 marks] AO4 [4 marks]**

Willy Russell: *Blood Brothers*

`0` `3` How does Russell use the character of Eddie to explore ideas about class?
Write about:
- how Russell presents Eddie
- how Russell uses these things to explore the theme of class.   **[30 marks] AO4 [4 marks]**

`0` `4` How does Russell present the theme of depression?
Write about:
- the ideas about depression in the play
- how Russell presents these ideas by the way he writes.   **[30 marks] AO4 [4 marks]**

Alan Bennett: *The History Boys*

`0` `5` How does Bennett present the relationship between Dakin and Scripps?
Write about:
- the things that Dakin and Scripps discuss
- how Bennett uses these things to show their friendship.   **[30 marks] AO4 [4 marks]**

`0` `6` How does Bennett explore the theme of reputation?
Write about:
- what different characters say and feel about reputation
- how Bennett uses this to explore ideas about reputation.   **[30 marks] AO4 [4 marks]**

Shelagh Delaney: *A Taste of Honey*

0 7 How does Delaney present the relationship between Jo and Geoffrey?
Write about:
- the relationship between Jo and Geoffrey
- how Delaney presents their relationship by the way she writes. **[30 marks] AO4 [4 marks]**

0 8 How does Delaney use Helen and Peter to explore ideas about gender?
Write about:
- ideas about gender explored through Helen and Peter
- how Delaney presents these ideas by the way she writes. **[30 marks] AO4 [4 marks]**

Simon Stephens: *The Curious Incident of the Dog in the Night-time*

0 9 How does Stephens present Judy as a parent?
Write about:
- the character of Judy and her relationship with Christopher
- how Stephens presents her as a parent by the way he writes. **[30 marks] AO4 [4 marks]**

1 0 How does Stephens explore the theme of communication?
Write about:
- the theme of communication in the play
- how Stephens presents this theme by the way he writes. **[30 marks] AO4 [4 marks]**

Dennis Kelly: *DNA*

1 1 How does Kelly present the characters of Jan and Mark?
Write about:
- the characters of Jan and Mark
- how Kelly presents these characters by the way he writes. **[30 marks] AO4 [4 marks]**

1 2 How does Kelly make use of monologues?
Write about:
- monologues in the play
- how Kelly makes effective use of these monologues. **[30 marks] AO4 [4 marks]**

William Golding: *Lord Of The Flies*

1 3 Do you think Simon is an important character in the novel?
Write about:
- how Golding presents the character of Simon
- how Golding uses Simon to present different themes in the novel. **[30 marks] AO4 [4 marks]**

1 4 How does Golding explore the theme of savagery?
Write about:
- which characters display savagery
- how Golding uses this to explore the theme of savagery. **[30 marks] AO4 [4 marks]**

George Orwell: *Animal Farm*

1 5 How does Orwell use Snowball and Napoleon to explore different ideas about leadership?
Write about:
- how Orwell presents Snowball's style of leadership
- how Orwell presents Napoleon's style of leadership. **[30 marks] AO4 [4 marks]**

| 1 | 6 | How does the ending summarise the ideas that Orwell is trying to explore in the novel?

Write about:
- how Orwell presents his ideas at the end of the novel
- how Orwell presents these ideas elsewhere in the novel.   **[30 marks] AO4 [4 marks]**

Kazuo Ishiguro: *Never Let Me Go*

| 1 | 7 | How does Ishiguro present the friendship between Kathy and Ruth?

Write about:
- how Ishiguro presents the strengths in their friendship
- how Ishiguro presents the weaknesses in their friendship.   **[30 marks] AO4 [4 marks]**

| 1 | 8 | How does Ishiguro present the theme of nostalgia?

Write about:
- which characters are nostalgic
- how Ishiguro uses this to explore his ideas.   **[30 marks] AO4 [4 marks])**

Meera Syal: *Anita And Me*

| 1 | 9 | How does Syal present the relationship between Meena and her Papa?

Write about:
- how Meena thinks and behaves towards Papa
- how Papa thinks and behaves towards Meena.   **[30 marks] AO4 [4 marks]**

| 2 | 0 | How does Syal present the theme of rebellion?

Write about:
- which characters are rebellious
- how Syal uses this to explore her ideas.   **[30 marks] AO4 [4 marks]**

Stephen Kelman: *Pigeon English*

| 2 | 1 | How does Kelman present the character of Harri's mother?

Write about:
- The character of Harri's mother
- How Kelman presents Harri's mother by the way he writes.   **[30 marks] AO4 [4 marks]**

| 2 | 2 | How does Kelman explore the theme of growing up?

Write about:
- the theme of growing up in *Pigeon English*
- how Kelman presents this theme by the way he writes.   **[30 marks] AO4 [4 marks]**

AQA Anthology: *Telling Tales*

| 2 | 3 | How do writers explore relationships between parents and children in 'A Family Supper' and one other story from *Telling Tales*?

Write about:
- relationships between parents and children in the two stories
- how the writers present these relationships by the way they write.   **[30 marks] AO4 [4 marks]**

| 2 | 4 | How do writers use symbolism and imagery in 'The Darkness Out There' and one other story from *Telling Tales*?

Write about:
- symbols and images in the two stories
- how their use helps to create meaning and affects the reader.   **[30 marks] AO4 [4 marks]**

Section B: Poetry
Answer **one** question from this section.
(Write your answers on a separate piece of paper.)

AQA Anthology: Poems Past and Present

EITHER

Love and Relationships

2 5   Compare how poets present attitudes towards the opposite sex in 'Sonnet 29 – I Think of Thee' and in one other poem from 'Love and Relationships'.

> I think of thee!—my thoughts do twine and bud
> About thee, as wild vines, about a tree,
> Put out broad leaves, and soon there's nought to see
> Except the straggling green which hides the wood.
> 5   Yet, O my palm-tree, be it understood
> I will not have my thoughts instead of thee
> Who art dearer, better! Rather, instantly
> Renew thy presence; as a strong tree should,
> Rustle thy boughs and set thy trunk all bare,
> 10   And let these bands of greenery which insphere thee
> Drop heavily down, —burst, shattered, everywhere!
> Because, in this deep joy to see and hear thee
> And breathe within thy shadow a new air,
> I do not think of thee—I am too near thee.

[30 marks]

Conflict and Power

2 **6** Compare the ways poets present ideas about war in 'The Charge of the Light Brigade' and in one other poem from 'Conflict and Power'.

1.
Half a league, half a league,
Half a league onward,
All in the valley of Death
   Rode the six hundred.
5 "Forward, the Light Brigade!
Charge for the guns!" he said.
Into the valley of Death
   Rode the six hundred.
   2.
"Forward, the Light Brigade!"
10 Was there a man dismaye'd?
Not though the soldier knew
   Some one had blunder'd.
Theirs not to make reply,
Theirs not to reason why,
15 Theirs but to do and die.
Into the valley of Death
   Rode the six hundred.
   3.
Cannon to right of them,
Cannon to left of them,
20 Cannon in front of them
   Volley'd and thunder'd;
Storm'd at with shot and shell,
Boldly they rode and well,
Into the jaws of Death,
25 Into the mouth of Hell
   Rode the six hundred.

   4.
Flash'd all their sabres bare,
Flash'd as they turn'd in air
Sabring the gunners there,
30 Charging an army, while
   All the world wonder'd.
Plunged in the battery-smoke
Right thro' the line they broke;
Cossack and Russian
35 Reel'd from the sabre-stroke
Shatter'd and sunder'd.
Then they rode back, but not
   Not the six hundred.
   5.
Cannon to right of them,
40 Cannon to left of them,
Cannon behind them
   Volley'd and thunder'd;
Stormed at with shot and shell,
While horse and hero fell.
45 They that had fought so well
Came thro' the jaws of Death
Back from the mouth of Hell,
All that was left of them,
   Left of six hundred.
   6.
50 When can their glory fade?
O the wild charge they made!
   All the world wonder'd.
Honour the charge they made!
Honour the Light Brigade,
55   Noble six hundred!

[30 marks]

Section C: Unseen Poetry

Answer **both** questions in this section.

(Write your answers on a separate piece of paper.)

27.1 In 'Hawk Roosting', how does the poet present ideas and feelings about hawks? **[24 marks]**

27.2 In both 'Hawk Roosting' and 'The Owl's Request', the poets convey their ideas and feelings about birds. What are the similarities and differences between the ways the poets present these ideas and feelings? **[8 marks]**

'Hawk Roosting'
by *Ted Hughes*

I sit in the top of the wood, my eyes closed.
Inaction, no falsifying dream
Between my hooked head and hooked feet:
Or in sleep rehearse perfect kills and eat.

The convenience of the high trees!
The air's buoyancy and the sun's ray
Are of advantage to me;
And the earth's face upward for my inspection.

My feet are locked upon the rough bark.
It took the whole of Creation
To produce my foot, my each feather:
Now I hold Creation in my foot

Or fly up, and revolve it all slowly -
I kill where I please because it is all mine.
There is no sophistry in my body:
My manners are tearing off heads -

The allotment of death.
For the one path of my flight is direct
Through the bones of the living.
No arguments assert my right:

The sun is behind me.
Nothing has changed since I began.
My eye has permitted no change.
I am going to keep things like this.

'The Owl's Request'
by *Elizabeth Jennings*

Do not be frightened of me.
I am a night-time creature. When the earth is still,
When trees are shadows of shadows,
When only the moon and its attendant stars
Enlarge the night, when the smallest sound is shrill
And may wake you up and frighten you,
I am about with my friendly, 'Tu-whit, tu whoo'.

My face is kindly but also mysterious.
People call me wise.
Perhaps they do so because I sometimes close my eyes
And seem to be thinking.
The way I think is not like yours. I need
No thick philosopher's book;
I can tell the truth of the world with a look
But I do not speak about
What I see there. Think of me then
As the certainty in your wandering nights.
I can soothe men
And will snatch you out of your doubt,
Bear you away to the stars and the moon
And to sleep and dawn. So lie
And listen to my lullaby.

PAGES 4–6

1. c, e, f, h

2. 1-2 marks = simple awareness of characters with some reference to texts; 3-4 marks = identifies a few points of comparison, supported by some quotations but sometimes generalise; 5-6 marks = clear comparison of characters with relevant quotations; 7-8 marks = full comparison of range of characteristics, well supported by quotations.

3. 1-3 marks = simple awareness of language with a few references to the text; 4-6 marks = some understanding how language is used, supported by some quotations; 7-9 marks = clear understanding of how language is used to achieve effects, supported by quotations; 10-12 marks = full understanding of how language is used to achieve effects, well supported by quotations.

4. 1-4 marks = simple awareness of different feelings/attitudes with a few references to the texts; 5-8 marks = identifies several different feelings/attitudes and tries to compare and to offer some comments on writers' techniques, supported by some quotations; 9-12 marks = clear understanding and comparison of different feelings/attitudes and how they are conveyed, with quotations as evidence; 13-16 marks = full comparison of different feelings/attitudes and the varied ways in which they are conveyed, well supported by quotations.

PAGES 7–9

1. b, c, f, g.

2. 1 mark = simple awareness of reasons through quotation; 2 marks = identifies a few reasons in own words but sometimes generalised; 3 marks = clear understanding of specific reasons; 4 marks = full understanding of specific reasons, well expressed.

3. 1 mark = simple awareness of setting through quotation; 2 marks = identifies a few points about setting in own words but sometimes generalised; 3 marks = clear understanding of specific features of setting; 4 marks = full understanding of setting, well expressed.

4. 1-3 marks = simple awareness of language with a few references to the text; 4-6 marks = some understanding of how language is used, supported by some quotations; 7-9 marks = clear understanding of how language is used to achieve effects, supported by quotations; 10-12 marks = full understanding of how language is used to achieve effects, well supported by quotations.

5. 1-4 marks = simple awareness of different feelings/attitudes with a few references to the texts; 5-8 marks = identifies several different feelings/attitudes and tries to compare and to offer some comments on writers' techniques, supported by some quotations; 9-12 marks = clear understanding and comparison of different feelings/ attitudes and how they are conveyed, with quotations as evidence; 13-16 marks = full comparison of different feelings/attitudes and the varied ways in which they are conveyed, well supported by quotations

PAGES 10–11

1. One mark, up to four marks, for each point about the gatekeeper.

2. 1-2 marks = simple understanding of language, with a few references to the text; 3-4 marks = some understanding of how language is being used, supported by quotations; 5-6 marks = clear understanding of how language is used to achieve some effects, supported by relevant quotations; 7-8 marks = full understanding of how language is used to achieve a range of effects, well supported by quotations.

3. 1-2 marks = simple understanding of narrative structure, with a few references to the text; 3-4 marks = some understanding of narrative structure and links to the audience, supported by quotations; 5-6 marks = clear understanding of how narrative structure engages the audience, supported by relevant quotations; 7-8 marks = full understanding of how narrative structure engages the audience, well supported by quotations.

4. 1-5 marks = simple comments on character, with a few references to the text; 6-10 marks = some evaluative comments about characterisation and writers' techniques, supported by quotations; 11-15 marks = clear evaluation of characterisation and writers' techniques, supported by relevant quotations; 16-20 marks = full evaluation of characterisation and writers' techniques, well supported by quotations.

PAGES 12–13

1. One mark, up to four marks, for each point about Ennis.

2. 1-2 marks = simple understanding of language, with a few references to the text; 3-4 marks = some understanding of how language is being used, supported by quotations; 5-6 marks = clear understanding of how language is used to achieve some effects, supported by relevant quotations; 7-8 marks = full understanding of how language is used to achieve a range of effects, well supported by quotations.

3. 1-2 marks = simple understanding of narrative structure, with a few references to the text; 3-4 marks = some understanding of narrative structure and links to the audience, supported by quotations; 5-6 marks = clear understanding of how narrative structure engages the audience, supported by relevant quotations; 7-8 marks = full understanding of how narrative structure engages the audience, well supported by quotations.

4. 1-5 marks = simple comments on character, with a few references to the text; 6-10 marks = some evaluative comments about characterisation and writers' techniques, supported by quotations; 11-15 marks = clear evaluation of characterisation and writers' techniques, supported by relevant quotations; 16-20 marks = full evaluation of characterisation and writers' techniques, well supported by quotations.

PAGES 14–15

1. One mark, up to four marks, for each point about the castle.

2. 1-2 marks = simple understanding of language, with a few references to the text; 3-4 marks = some understanding of how language is being used, supported by quotations; 5-6 marks = clear understanding of how language is used to achieve some effects, supported by relevant quotations; 7-8 marks = full understanding of how language is used to achieve a range of effects, well supported by quotations.

3. 1-2 marks = simple understanding of narrative structure, with a few references to the text; 3-4 marks = some understanding of narrative structure and links to the audience, supported by quotations; 5-6 marks = clear understanding of how narrative structure engages the audience, supported by relevant quotations; 7-8 marks = full understanding of how narrative structure engages the audience, well supported by quotations.

4. 1-5 marks = simple comments on character, with a few references to the text; 6-10 marks = some evaluative comments about characterisation and writers' techniques, supported by quotations; 11-15 marks = clear evaluation of characterisation and writers' techniques, supported by relevant quotations; 16-20 marks = full evaluation of characterisation and writers' techniques, well supported by quotations.

PAGES 16–17

1. 'And now I come to the point where I met with such sudden and desperate disaster.'

2. 'the rock had been cut away and made top-heavy by the rush of the stream.'

3. 'more amused than alarmed by my adventure'/'but I had two others in my pocket, so that it was of no importance'.

4. 1-2 marks = simple understanding of language, with a few references to the text; 3-4 marks = some understanding of how language is being used, supported by quotations; 5-6 marks = clear understanding of how language is used to achieve some effects, supported by relevant quotations; 7-8 marks = full understanding of how language is used to achieve a range of effects, well supported by quotations.

5. 1-2 marks = simple understanding of narrative structure, with a few references to the text; 3-4 marks = some understanding of narrative structure and links to the audience, supported by quotations; 5-6 marks = clear understanding of how narrative structure engages the audience, supported by relevant quotations; 7-8 marks = full understanding of how narrative structure engages the audience, well supported by quotations.

6. 1-5 marks = simple comments on character and atmosphere, with a few references to the text; 6-10 marks = some evaluative comments about characterisation, atmosphere and writers' techniques, supported by quotations; 11-15 marks = clear evaluation of characterisation, creation of atmosphere and writers' techniques, supported by relevant quotations; 16-20 marks = full evaluation of characterisation, the creation of atmosphere and writers' techniques, well supported by quotations.

PAGE 18

1. a) there; their; they're. b) too; two; to. c) right; write

2. a) women b) keys c) juries d) sheep e) babies f) witches

3. a) compound b) complex c) simple

4. a) She's b) can't c) Marco's d) children's e) cats' f) Mary's

5. a) did b) gave c) carried d) going to e) eaten f) got

PAGES 19–25

All questions are marked out of 40: 24 marks for content and organisation, and 16 marks for technical accuracy (spelling, punctuation and grammar).

Content and organisation:

1–3 marks = One or two unlinked ideas; no paragraphs; communicates simple meaning; simple vocabulary; occasional sense of purpose, audience and/or form.

4–6 marks = One or two relevant ideas; some attempts to paragraph; communicates simple meanings successfully; simple vocabulary; basic awareness of purpose, audience and form.

7–9 marks = Some linked and relevant ideas; some successful paragraphs; communicates with some success; begins to vary vocabulary and use some linguistic devices; attempts to match purpose, audience and form.

10–12 marks = Increasing variety of linked and relevant ideas; some clear paragraphs; communication is mostly successful; some attempts to make use of vocabulary and linguistic devices; sustained attempt to match purpose, audience and form.

13–15 marks = range of connected and engaging ideas; usually clear paragraphs; communicates clearly; vocabulary and linguistic devices chosen for clear effect; successfully matches purpose, audience and form.

16–18 marks = range of detailed, connected and engaging ideas; clear, useful paragraphs; communication consistently clear and effective; some sophisticated vocabulary and some range of linguistic devices used effectively; tone, style and register match the purpose, audience and form.

19–21 marks = a range of structured, developed and engaging ideas; consistently effective paragraphing; communication is convincing; sophisticated vocabulary and linguistic devices show evidence of conscious crafting; tone, style, and register consistently match the purpose, audience and form.

22–24 marks = a range of highly structured, developed, complex and engaging ideas; fluently linked paragraphs are used to clarify and emphasise meaning; communication is convincing and compelling; extensive and ambitious vocabulary and linguistic devices show sustained crafting; tone, style, and register are subtly and consistently used to match purpose and form, and to affect the audience.

Technical accuracy (Spelling, Punctuation and Grammar):

1–4 marks = sentences occasionally marked out by full stops; simple range of sentences; occasional Standard English; accurate basic spelling.

5–8 marks = basic sentence structures usually secure; some punctuation within sentences; attempts a variety of sentences; some controlled Standard English; some accurate spelling of more complex words.

9–12 marks = sentences are mostly secure; range of punctuation used, generally with success; uses a variety of sentence forms for effect; mostly Standard English with controlled grammar; generally accurate spelling, including complex and irregular words.

13–16 mark = sentences are consistently secure; wide range of punctuation is used with accuracy; uses a full range of sentence forms for effect; Standard English is consistently used and more complex grammatical structures are used accurately; high level of accuracy in spelling, including ambitious vocabulary.

PAGES 26-27

1. 1 mark for explaining that a simile is a comparison that uses 'like' or 'as'; 2 further marks for finding an example and explaining the effect of the simile.

2. 1 mark for explaining that a metaphor is a comparison that is written as if it's true (not 'like' or 'as'); 2 further marks for finding an

example and explaining the effect of the metaphor.

3. 1 mark for explaining that personification is describing an object or idea as if it had human qualities; 2 further marks for finding an example and explaining the effect of the use of personification.

4. 1 mark for explaining that alliteration is the repetition of sounds at the start of a series of words; 2 further marks for finding an example and explaining the effect of the use of alliteration.

5. 1 mark for explaining that onomatopoeia is when words sound like the sound they describe; 2 further marks for finding an example and explaining the effect of the use of onomatopoeia.

6. 1 mark for explaining that rhyme is when words end with the same vowel and consonant sounds: 2 further marks for finding an example and explaining the effect of the rhyme.

7. a)–e) 1 mark for each example and 2 further marks for explaining the effect created by each example.

8. 1 mark for explaining that a persona is a character adopted by a poet writing in the first person; 2 further marks for finding an example and explaining the effect of the use of a persona.

9. 2 marks for a clear explanation of the Romantic movement (e.g.' It was a group of poets who wrote about emotions and nature, using traditional forms') and 4 marks for a clear explanation of how the chosen poem reflects the ideas of the Romantic movement.

PAGES 28- 31
All anthology questions marked out of 30.

1-4 marks – simple comments; one or two direct references to the poems; little or no comparison.

5-8 marks - relevant comments; several direct references to the poems; some reference to language and structure; some comparison.

9-16 marks – a range of relevant comments; some relevant quotations; identification and some explanation of language and structure techniques; some relevant comparison; awareness of context.

17-22 marks – clear sustained focus on the question; a range of relevant quotations; identification understanding of how language and structure convey meaning; a range of clear comparisons; some consideration of context.

23-26 marks – thoughtful and developed analysis; a range of well -integrated quotations; sustained analysis of how language, structure and form convey meaning; a range of thoughtful and developed comparisons; consideration of context and alternative interpretations.

27-30 marks – exploratory and evaluative analysis; a range of well- integrated quotations; sustained and sophisticated analysis of how language, structure and form convey meaning; a full range of thoughtful and developed comparisons; convincing use of contextual factors and alternative interpretations.

PAGES 32-39
Each pair of unseen poetry questions is marked out of 32 (24 for the first question and 8 for the second)

1. (qs 1,3,5 & 7)

   1-4 marks – simple comments; one or two direct references to the poems; some awareness of language.

   5-8 marks - relevant comments; several direct references to the poems; some reference to language

and/or structure.

9-12 marks – a range of relevant comments; some relevant quotations; identification and some explanation of language and/or structure techniques.

13-16 marks – clear sustained focus on the question; a range of relevant quotations; identification and understanding of how language and structure convey meaning.

17-20 marks – thoughtful and developed analysis; a range of well-integrated quotations; sustained analysis of how language, structure and form convey meaning.

21-24 marks – exploratory and evaluative analysis; a range of well-integrated quotations; sustained and sophisticated analysis of how language, structure and form convey meaning.

2. (qs 2,4,6 & 8)

   1-2 marks – simple comments; awareness of similarities and differences; one or two references to the texts; simple awareness of language.

   3-4 marks – a range of comments; some focus on comparison; some relevant quotations; identification and explanation of language and structure/form.

   5-6 marks – thoughtful analysis; thoughtful and developed comparison; a range of well-integrated quotations; sustained analysis of how language and structure/form convey meaning.

   7-8 marks – exploratory and evaluative analysis and comparison; a range of well-integrated quotations; sustained and sophisticated analysis of how language, structure and form convey meaning.

PAGES 40–51
All Shakespeare questions are marked out of a total of 30.

1–5 marks = simple comments; one or two direct references to the text; simple awareness of language.

6–10 marks = relevant comments; some focus on the question; direct references to the text; some reference to techniques of language and/or structure.

11–15 marks = a range of points; focus on the question; some relevant quotations; identification and explanation of some techniques of language and/or structure.

16–20 marks = clear, sustained focus on the question; a range of quotations; understanding of how different techniques of language, structure and/or form convey meaning; some consideration of contextual factors.

21–25 marks = thoughtful and developed analysis; a range of well-integrated quotations; sustained analysis of how a variety of different techniques of language, structure and/or form convey meaning; consideration of contextual factors and alternative interpretations.

26–30 marks = exploratory and evaluative analysis; a range of well-integrated quotations; sustained analysis of how a full range of techniques of language, structure and form convey meaning; convincing use of contextual factors and alternative interpretations.

PAGE 52

1. 1 mark for correct identification of first person/third person narrator; 2 marks for omniscient/intrusive/naïve/unreliable.

2. 2 marks for correct identification (Pip/Scrooge/Elizabeth/Jane Eyre/Sherlock Holmes/Frankenstein).

3. 2 marks for each valid point, up to a maximum of 10 marks.

4. 1 mark for each character identified and 1 for an explanation, up to a maximum of 10 marks.
5. 1 mark for each place identified and 1 for an explanation, up to a maximum of 10 marks.
6. 2 marks for each incident, up to a maximum of 10 marks.

PAGES 53–59

All 19th Century Novel questions are marked out of 30 (15 marks for each of the two sections).

1–5 marks = simple comments; one or two direct references to the text; simple awareness of language.

6–10 marks = relevant comments; some focus on the question; direct references to the text; some reference to techniques of language and/or structure.

11–15 marks = a range of points; focus on the question; some relevant quotations; identification and explanation of some techniques of language and/or structure.

16–20 marks = clear, sustained focus on the question; a range of quotations; understanding of how different techniques of language, structure and/or form convey meaning; some consideration of contextual factors.

21–25 marks = thoughtful and developed analysis; a range of well-integrated quotations; sustained analysis of how a variety of different techniques of language, structure and/or form convey meaning; consideration of contextual factors and alternative interpretations.

26–30 marks = exploratory and evaluative analysis; a range of well-integrated quotations; sustained analysis of how a full range of techniques of language, structure and form convey meaning; convincing use of contextual factors and alternative interpretations.

PAGES 60–63

All Modern Texts questions are marked out of 30.

1–4 marks = simple comments; one or two direct references to the text; simple awareness of language.

5–8 marks = relevant comments; some focus on the question; direct references to the text; some reference to techniques of language and/or structure.

9–16 marks = a range of points; focus on the question; some relevant quotations; identification and explanation of some techniques of language and/or structure.

17–22 marks = clear, sustained focus on the question; a range of quotations; understanding of how different techniques of language, structure and/or form convey meaning; some consideration of contextual factors.

23–26 marks = thoughtful and developed analysis; a range of well-integrated quotations; sustained analysis of how a variety of different techniques of language, structure and/or form convey meaning; consideration of contextual factors and alternative interpretations.

27–30 marks = exploratory and evaluative analysis; a range of well-integrated quotations; sustained analysis of how a full range of techniques of language, structure and form convey meaning; convincing use of contextual factors and alternative interpretations.

PAGES 64–66

1. One mark, up to four marks, for each point about the narrator's gratitude.
2. 1–2 marks = simple awareness of language and/or structure, with a few references to the text; 3–4 marks = some understanding of how language and/or structure is being used, supported by some quotations; 5–6 marks = clear understanding of how language and structure have been used to achieve some effects, with quotations as evidence; 7–8 marks = full understanding of how language and structure have been used to achieve various effects, well-supported by quotations.
3. 1–2 marks = simple awareness of narrative structure, such as start or end, with a few references to the text; 3–4 marks = some understanding of the narrative structure and links to audience, supported by some quotations; 5–6 marks = clear understanding of how the narrative structure engages the reader, with quotations as evidence; 7–8 marks = full understanding of how the narrative structure engages the reader, well-supported by quotations.
4. 1–5 marks = simple comments on character, with a few references to the text; 6–10 marks = some evaluative comments about characterisation and writer's techniques, supported by some quotation; 11–15 marks = clear evaluation of characterisation and writer's techniques, with quotations as evidence; 16–20 marks = full evaluation of characterisation and a range of writer's techniques, well-supported by quotations.
5. Content and organisation:

   1–3 marks = One or two unlinked ideas; no paragraphs; communicates simple meaning; simple vocabulary; occasional sense of purpose, audience and/or form.

   4–6 marks = One or two relevant ideas; some attempts to paragraph; communicates simple meanings successfully; simple vocabulary; basic awareness of purpose, audience and form.

   7–9 marks = Some linked and relevant ideas; some successful paragraphs; communicates with some success; begins to vary vocabulary and use some linguistic devices; attempts to match purpose, audience and form.

   10–12 marks = Increasing variety of linked and relevant ideas; some clear paragraphs; communication is mostly successful; some attempts to make use of vocabulary and linguistic devices; sustained attempt to match purpose, audience and form.

   13–15 marks = range of connected and engaging ideas; usually clear paragraphs; communicates clearly; vocabulary and linguistic devices chosen for clear effect; successfully matches purpose, audience and form.

   16–18 marks = range of detailed, connected and engaging ideas; clear, useful paragraphs; communication consistently clear and effective; some sophisticated vocabulary and some range of linguistic devices used effectively; tone, style and register match the purpose, audience and form.

   19–21 marks = a range of structured, developed and engaging ideas; consistently effective paragraphing; communication is convincing; sophisticated vocabulary and linguistic devices show evidence of conscious crafting; tone, style, and register consistently match the purpose, audience and form.

   22–24 marks = a range of highly structured, developed, complex and engaging ideas; fluently linked paragraphs are used to clarify and emphasise meaning; communication is convincing and compelling; extensive and ambitious vocabulary and linguistic devices show sustained crafting; tone, style, and register are subtly and consistently used to match purpose and form, and to affect the audience.

   Technical accuracy (Spelling, Punctuation and Grammar):

   1–4 marks = sentences occasionally marked out by full stops; simple range of sentences; occasional Standard English; accurate basic spelling.

   5–8 marks = basic sentence structures usually secure; some punctuation within sentences; attempts a variety of sentences; some controlled Standard English; some accurate spelling of more complex words.

   9–12 marks = sentences are mostly secure; range of punctuation used, generally with success; uses a variety of sentence forms for effect; mostly Standard English with controlled grammar; generally accurate spelling, including complex and irregular words.

   13–16 marks = sentences are consistently secure; wide range of punctuation is used with accuracy; uses a full range of sentence forms for effect; Standard English is consistently used and more complex grammatical structures are used accurately; high level of accuracy in spelling, including ambitious vocabulary.

PAGES 67–70

1. A, C, D, H

2. 1–2 marks = simple awareness of attitudes in both texts with some reference to the texts; 3–4 marks = identifies a few points of comparison, supported by some quotations, but sometimes generalised; 5–6 marks = clear comparison of attitudes, with quotations; 7–8 marks = full comparison of attitudes, well-supported by quotations.

3. 1–3 marks = simple awareness of language, with a few references to the text; 4–6 marks = some understanding of how language is being used, supported by some quotations; 7–9 marks = clear understanding of how language has been used to achieve some effects, with quotations as evidence; 10–12 marks = full understanding of how language has been used to achieve various effects, well-supported by quotations.

4. 1–4 marks = simple awareness of different attitudes, with a few references to the texts; 5–8 marks = identifies several different attitudes and tries to compare as well as offer some comments on writers' techniques, supported by some quotations; 9–12 marks = clear understanding and comparison of different attitudes and how they are conveyed, with quotations as evidence; 13–16 marks = full comparison of different attitudes and the varied ways in which they have been conveyed, well–supported by quotations.

5. Content and organisation:

    1–3 marks = One or two unlinked ideas; no paragraphs; communicates simple meaning; simple vocabulary; occasional sense of purpose, audience and/or form.

    4–6 marks = One or two relevant ideas; some attempts to paragraph; communicates simple meanings successfully; simple vocabulary; basic awareness of purpose, audience and form.

    7–9 marks = Some linked and relevant ideas; some successful paragraphs; communicates with some success; begins to vary vocabulary and use some linguistic devices; attempts to match purpose, audience and form.

    10–12 marks = Increasing variety of linked and relevant ideas; some clear paragraphs; communication is mostly successful; some attempts to make use of vocabulary and linguistic devices; sustained attempt to match purpose, audience and form.

    13–15 marks = range of connected and engaging ideas; usually clear paragraphs; communicates clearly; vocabulary and linguistic devices chosen for clear effect; successfully matches purpose, audience and form.

    16–18 marks = range of detailed, connected and engaging ideas; clear, useful paragraphs; communication consistently clear and effective; some sophisticated vocabulary and some range of linguistic devices used effectively; tone, style and register match the purpose, audience and form.

    19–21 marks = a range of structured, developed and engaging ideas; consistently effective paragraphing; communication is convincing; sophisticated vocabulary

and linguistic devices show evidence of conscious crafting; tone, style, and register consistently match the purpose, audience and form.

22–24 marks = a range of highly structured, developed, complex and engaging ideas; fluently linked paragraphs are used to clarify and emphasise meaning; communication is convincing and compelling; extensive and ambitious vocabulary and linguistic devices show sustained crafting; tone, style, and register are subtly and consistently used to match purpose and form, and to affect the audience.

Technical accuracy (Spelling, Punctuation and Grammar):

1–4 marks = sentences occasionally marked out by full stops; simple range of sentences; occasional Standard English; accurate basic spelling.

5–8 marks = basic sentence structures usually secure; some punctuation within sentences; attempts a variety of sentences; some controlled Standard English; some accurate spelling of more complex words.

9–12 marks = sentences are mostly secure; range of punctuation used, generally with success; uses a variety of sentence forms for effect; mostly Standard English with controlled grammar; generally accurate spelling, including complex and irregular words.

13–16 marks = sentences are consistently secure; wide range of punctuation is used with accuracy; uses a full range of sentence forms for effect; Standard English is consistently used and more complex grammatical structures are used accurately; high level of accuracy in spelling, including ambitious vocabulary.

PAGES 71–86

All Shakespeare, 19th Century Novel and Modern Text questions are marked out of 30.(Questions **1.–24.**)

1–5 marks = simple comments; one or two direct references to the text; simple awareness of language.

6–10 marks = relevant comments; some focus on the question; direct references to the text; some reference to techniques of language and/or structure.

11–15 marks = a range of points; focus on the question; some relevant quotations; identification and explanation of some techniques of language and/or structure.

16–20 marks = clear, sustained focus on the question; a range of quotations; understanding of how different techniques of language, structure and/or form convey meaning; some consideration of contextual factors.

21–25 marks = thoughtful and developed analysis; a range of well-integrated quotations; sustained analysis of how a variety of different techniques of language, structure and/or form convey meaning; consideration of contextual factors and alternative interpretations.

26–30 marks = exploratory and evaluative analysis; a range of well-integrated quotations; sustained analysis of how a full range of techniques of language, structure and form convey meaning; convincing use of contextual factors and alternative interpretations.

Additional spelling, punctuation, and grammar marks for the Shakespeare and Modern Text questions: 1 mark for some accuracy and mostly clear meaning; 2 marks for reasonable accuracy and fully clear meaning; 3 marks for considerable accuracy and written control; 4 marks for consistently accurate and effectively controlled writing.

25.–26. The Anthology poetry questions are marked
out of 30.

1–5 marks = simple comments; awareness of similarity and
difference; one or two direct references to the poems; simple
awareness of language.

6–10 marks = relevant comments; some comparisons; direct
references to the poems; some reference to techniques of language
and/or structure.

11–15 marks = a range of points; some focus on comparison;
some relevant quotations; identification and explanation of some
techniques of language and/or structure.

16–20 marks = clear, sustained focus on the question; clear,
sustained comparison; a range of quotations; understanding of
how different techniques of language, structure and/or form convey
meaning; some consideration of contextual factors.

21–25 marks = thoughtful, developed analysis and comparison;
a range of well-integrated quotations; sustained analysis of how a
variety of different techniques of language, structure and/or form
convey meaning; consideration of contextual factors and alternative
interpretations.

26–30 marks = exploratory, evaluative analysis and comparison;
a range of well-integrated quotations; sustained analysis of how a
full range of techniques of language, structure and form convey
meaning; convincing use of contextual factors and alternative
interpretations.

27.1 The single unseen poetry question is marked out of 24.
1–4 marks = simple comments; one or two direct references to the
poem; simple awareness of language.

5–8 marks = relevant comments; direct references to the poem;
some reference to techniques of language and/or structure.

9–12 marks = a range of points; some relevant quotations;
identification and explanation of some techniques of language and/
or structure.

13–16 marks = clear, sustained focus on the question; a range of
quotations; understanding of how different techniques of language,
structure and/or form convey meaning.

17–20 marks = thoughtful and developed analysis; a range of
well-integrated quotations; sustained analysis of how a variety of
different techniques of language, structure and/or form convey
meaning.

21–24 marks = exploratory and evaluative analysis; a range of
well-integrated quotations; sustained analysis of how a full range of
techniques of language, structure and form convey meaning.

27.2 The unseen poetry comparison is marked out of 8.

1–2 marks = simple, relevant comments; some comparisons;
direct references to the poems; some reference to techniques of
language and/or structure.

3–4 marks = a range of points focussed on the question; clear,
sustained comparison; a range of quotations; clear explanation of
how different techniques of language, structure and/or form convey
meaning.

5–6 marks = thoughtful, developed analysis and comparison;
a range of well-integrated quotations; analysis of how different
techniques of language, structure and/or form convey meaning.

7–8 marks = exploratory, evaluative comparison; a range of
well-integrated quotations; sustained analysis of how a range of
techniques of language, structure and form convey meaning.

Acknowledgements

P.4 From *Auto Da Fay by Fay* Weldon. Reprinted by permission of HarperCollins Publishers Ltd © Fay Weldon, 2002.

P.5 From Thoughts on Cheapness and My Aunt Charlotte by H G Wells. (A P Watt at United Agents on behalf of the Literary Executors of the Estate of H G Wells.)

P.7 'Melbourne in the Moonlight: a nighttime kayak tour' by Beverley Fearis, Friday 4th April, 2014.

P.10-11 From *The Falls* by Joyce Carol Oates. Reprinted by permission of HarperCollins Publishers Ltd © Joyce Carol Oates, 2004.

P.12 From *Brokeback Mountain* by Annie Proulx. © Dead Line Ltd 1997. Reproduced by kind permission of the Author and The Sayle Literary Agency.

P.34 '*Returning We Hear the Larks*' From *Collected Poems* by *Isaac Rosenberg*. (Published by Chatto & Windus.) (The Random House Group Ltd.)

P.33 *Funeral Blues* Copyright © 1991 by W H Auden, renewed. Reprinted by permission of Curtis Brown, Ltd.

P.36 'In Mrs Tilscher's Class' from The Other Country by Carol Ann Duffy. Published by Anvil Press Poetry, 1990. Copyright © Carol Ann Duffy. Reproduced by permission of the author c/o Rogers, Coleridge & White Ltd., 20 Powis Mews, London W11 1JN

P.39 'The Trees' by Philip Larkin, from *Collected Poems* (Faber and Faber Ltd.)

P.64 From *Unless* © 4th Estate, 2010, Carol Shields.

P.67 Extract from *Who* on Earth is Tom Baker? by Tom Baker, published by HarperCollins © Tom Baker 1997. Reproduced by permission of Sheil Land Associates Ltd.

P.89 'Hawk Roosting' by Ted Hughes, from *Collected Poems* (Faber and Faber Ltd.)

P.89 'The Owl's Request' by Elizabeth Jennings, from *A Spell of Words* (Macmillan, 1997).